LISTEN FOR GOD'S LEADING

LISTEN FOR GOD'S LEADING

**A Workbook for
Corporate Spiritual
Discernment**

Valerie K. Isenhower

Judith A. Todd

UPPER ROOM BOOKS®
NASHVILLE

The Upper Room® Web site: http://www.upperroom.org

UPPER ROOM®, UPPER ROOM BOOKS®, and design logos are trademarks owned by The Upper Room®, A Ministry of GBOD®, Nashville, Tennessee. All rights reserved.

Scripture quotations are from the New Revised Standard Version Bible, copyright 1989, Division of Christian Education of the National Council of the Churches of Christ in the United States of America. Used by permission. All rights reserved.

Scripture noted AT is the author's translation.

The exercises in appendix B were originally published in *Living into the Answers: A Workbook for Personal Spiritual Discernment*. Copyright © 2008 by Valerie K. Isenhower and Judith A. Todd. Used by permission of Upper Room Books.

Excerpt from Janet Cawley, *Who Is Our Church?* (Herndon, VA: Alban Institute, 2006) used by permission.

At the time of publication, all Web sites referenced in this book were valid. However, due to the fluid nature of the Internet, some addresses may have changed, or the content may no longer be relevant.

Cover and interior design: Gore Studio, Inc., Nashville / www.gorestudio.com
Cover photo: V. Isenhower Photography
First printing: 2009

Library of Congress Cataloging-in-Publication Data

Isenhower, Valerie K.
   Listen for God's leading: a workbook for corporate spiritual discernment /
Valerie K. Isenhower, Judith A. Todd
          p. cm.
      Includes bibliographical references.
      ISBN 978-0-8358-9985-7
1. Discernment (Christian theology)—Study and teaching. 2. Church—Study and teaching
2. I. Todd, Judith A.   II. Title
   BV4509.5.I834 2008
   268—dc22
         2008026361

Printed in the United States of America

CONTENTS

ACKNOWLEDGMENTS

We, the leaders of Water in the Desert Ministries, have been doing spiritual discernment in our own lives for years, including teaching it to others. We wish to thank many people for their contributions to the study of spiritual discernment. These individuals have added to our understanding of the subject. We are grateful to Danny Morris, Chuck Olsen, and Ellen Morseth for their contribution to the study of corporate spiritual discernment as it can make a difference in the church today. Graham Standish and Vicki Curtiss have continued the work of discernment and placing God in the center of church business. Even though spiritual discernment is an ancient practice, these individuals have contributed much toward its application in our own day. Their books are listed in the bibliography.

We also wish to express our gratitude to Ingrid Dvirnak and others who have read this workbook in its early stages and have offered suggestions and comments to make it clearer and easier to use. We are encouraged by those people who have been willing to field-test the process. We give thanks to the Reverend Shelley Craig and the team at Trinity Presbyterian Church in Topeka, Kansas, especially as they have contributed to clarification of the ways we can approach discernment in our lives and congregations.

We give thanks for Robin Pippin, editorial director for Upper Room Books, and Jeannie Crawford-Lee, our project manager. Robin believed in us and our work when she read our manuscripts, and Jeannie's editorial work has been very helpful. Our thanks also go to everyone at Upper Room Books for their work on this book.

INTRODUCTION

Thank you for choosing a workbook on spiritual discernment for your church. Our prayer is that this workbook becomes a practical tool for faith-based decision making in your church or organization. Discernment practices have been an important part of our faith journeys at Water in the Desert Ministries. We are committed to practicing discernment in our individual lives and as we plan and grow as an organization. We understand this process to be a major part of the life of mature Christians.

We have come to realize that many people are writing about or leading workshops on Christian spiritual practices, and still others are addressing peace and justice issues. We understand that devoting time and energy to discerning the leading of the Holy Spirit needs to be part of both arenas. We heard a call to use our years of experience and research to write workbooks on the process of incorporating spirituality with active participation in social change. These two sides of the life of discipleship strengthen and support both personal and corporate discernment.

Before reading any further: stop, take three deep breaths, and offer the reading and the process of discernment to God. Ask for God's guidance and grace as you begin the journey that lies ahead.

Purpose of the Workbook

Discernment is a way of listening and paying attention to God's leading. Discernment helps us seek God's vision for our church or organization and the directions for its ministry. This workbook is intended to be a guide to your corporate spiritual journeys. This presentation gives you practical tools to discover God's yearning for your church or organization, and at the same it time undergirds the process with in-depth spiritual formation.

If you have our workbook *Living into the Answers: A Workbook for Personal Spiritual Discernment* (Upper Room Books, 2008), you will notice many similarities. The two workbooks may be used as companion pieces for any group entering into the corporate discernment journey, and they do overlap. There is no question that corporate discernment is strengthened when the members of the organization practice discernment in their own lives.

Discernment calls upon the members of your church or organization to listen to God through the leading of the Holy Spirit, and to listen to one another. In this workbook we assume the leadership of your church is ready for change. You may be dissatisfied with strategic-planning results and asset-evaluation techniques. Or your church may be looking for a way of planning centered in faith and discipleship. The one area missing in most available inventories and guides is learning how to listen for God's leading. This workbook focuses on questions such as these:

> Who is God calling us to become as a community of faith?
> Where is Christ's presence active among us?
> Where is the Holy Spirit leading us?

The process contained here allows you to uncover God's longing for your church or organization. The movement of the Holy Spirit is often unseen but felt like the wind. Just as the wind moves hot air balloons, so the Holy Spirit can influence the process of movement in the church. The cover photograph, taken by Val at the Albuquerque International Balloon Fiesta, reminds us that God breathes dynamic life into our churches. The clouds in the photograph suggest the mystery and hiddenness of our flight. We, like hot air balloons, can sail with the wind into a God-breathed future. If you are ready for the transformative possibilities inherent in opening yourselves up to God's leading, then this workbook will provide direction and encouragement for the journey.

The discernment process is filled with prayer and worship, with discussion and interaction, with addressing issues and facing the challenges of your congregation's life together. The Albuquerque International Balloon Fiesta each year exemplifies the camaraderie of many balloons filling the air with color, shape, and texture. The discernment process can be accomplished through individual flight or, in a more exciting way, shared with others as new color, shape, and texture emerge for the church.

As you become more involved in corporate discernment practices, we recommend the individuals who are part of the process also choose to use *Living into the Answers: A Workbook for Personal Spiritual Discernment* for themselves. Small groups could be formed to use that workbook together. In this way, members of the planning group would learn to practice personal discernment as the whole body enters into the corporate discernment process. Such groups or discernment teams could then gather to discuss each movement of spiritual discernment and how they are applying it personally.

We also recommend that each person in the process read through the whole workbook before doing any of the exercises in order to have a sense of the flow of the different circles we describe. After reading through the workbook, return to chapter 1 to begin. Do not become overanxious or impatient and skip the first three chapters in order to get to the heart of the matter. You will build a foundation for the entire spiritual discernment process as you work through these early chapters. Also, resist the temptation to skip any of the individual steps. Know that if a decision is made to skip a portion of the workbook, the issues left unattended inevitably will surface and will need to be explored later.

Many people ask us about the frequency of meetings for the discernment team. We suggest meeting once a week or every other week, especially for the foundational sections. Meeting frequently builds momentum between sessions. Weekly meetings enhance the sense of community, which is important to the discernment process (see chapter 2), and the sessions can become a small-group spiritual experience for the members.

Lift up the process and those on the discernment team in prayer during worship.

As you proceed through the workbook, allow time for the suggested activities in the chapters to deepen your corporate journey. Use this workbook in conjunction with Bibles, pens, and perhaps journals for more extensive answers to the reflection questions and suggestions. You will also want to have newsprint, markers, and tape available for processing the activities on a larger scale in the group. Before each exercise, designate one person as leader for the activity. You may want to do this a week ahead of time so the individual can be prepared to lead. After each session, ask someone to type your discoveries and distribute the summary to the group. Keep the "used" newsprint and post pertinent sheets during future meetings.

The discernment process needs to permeate all that you are doing in the church. We suggest bringing some of the biblical themes of discernment into worship. Preach on the scriptural texts woven into this workbook. Lift up the process and those on the discernment team in prayer during worship. Add the process and your leaders to the prayer list. Offer Bible studies on discernment. Most importantly: stop, look, and listen to what is going on around you at the church during this time. It is amazing what will prove to be helpful.

Corporate spiritual discernment takes a long time. A church is like an ocean liner, and it takes time to turn a ship that large. Plan on the full process of discernment taking two to three years. Undoubtedly you will see changes and a difference in the life of the church before the process is completed. However, to shift the ways in which the church goes about its business, and to be faithful to all that spiritual discernment calls you to do, will take time. Don't rush. Give yourselves time to rest and find an appropriate rhythm for the changes along the way.

Discernment is not a linear process. Portions of the process described in the workbook may be repeated again and again. As the corporate issues become clearer, the focus for discussion will change. As groups explore areas of the church's life together more deeply, the group will participate in discernment at deeper levels. As the Holy Spirit guides discernment, the ability to uncover more of the roots and implications of the issues will be easier. Thus, repeating parts of the workbook becomes both necessary and important.

One desired outcome for spiritual discernment is to feel so comfortable with the process that it becomes a part of the life of your church or organization. Each decision presents an opportunity for living in God's presence more deeply.

May you be richly blessed as you explore spiritual discernment and listen for God's purposes for the life of your church or organization.

CHAPTER ONE

Corporate Discernment

Scripture: *Ephesians 4:11-12, 15-16*

The gifts [Christ] gave were that some would be apostles, some prophets, some evangelists, some pastors and teachers, to equip the saints for the work of ministry, for building up the body of Christ. . . . But speaking the truth in love, *we must grow up in every way into him who is the head, into Christ,* from whom the whole body, joined and knit together by every ligament with which it is equipped, as each part is working properly, promotes the body's growth in building itself up in love. (emphasis added)

Foundations

DISCERNMENT begins with God. According to Celia Hahn, "before discernment is deciding to do anything, it is being available to God."[1] Discernment begins with putting God in the center of everything that is done in the church, including decision making. Churches usually focus on issues such as membership, finances, and worship. The guides for decision making become the latest writings in church growth, worship, or organizational strategies. This workbook turns the decision-making processes in another direction. Discernment seeks to listen to God's yearning for the church *first,* placing corporate issues into a much larger perspective. Questions for discussion then arise in a shifted framework.

Because Christ is the head of the church, our decision making and visioning need to be Christ-centered. Our faith in Christ forms one fundamental difference between the church and secular business. The business world offers efficient and productive practices that have helped enterprises grow and thrive.

However, we cannot simply apply secular business practices to our life in the church. Chuck Olsen in *Transforming Church Boards into Communities of Spiritual Leaders* talks about the integration of spirituality and administration. He recovers the biblical paradigm for church leaders as spiritual leaders. The leaders become a community of Christ "with gifts and power to act."[2]

The Holy Spirit acts as our guide in spiritual discernment. John 14:26 says that "the Advocate [Guide], the Holy Spirit, whom the Father will send in my name, will teach you everything, and remind you of all that I have said to you." Therefore, decision making and planning in the church must be open to the leading of the Holy Spirit. The Spirit opens our hearts and minds to hearing and gives us the wisdom we need to seek God's vision.

Spiritual discernment leads to transformation. The church's relationship with the triune God will never be the same after beginning to seek a corporate life of discernment. Relationships among members and with people outside the church body will be deepened and strengthened as the relationships are seen in a different light. All the time the Spirit is moving and supporting and guiding the church into newness of life.

Actively engaging the triune God in the decision making of church boards taps into the power the Trinity offers to Christians. This power is freely given to us. We need only claim it through listening, paying attention, and acting on God's leading. To do anything less means we are acting out of our power rather than God's.

In speaking of God's will, we often imagine God opening up one path or having one purpose for us. When searching for God's will, it is easy to get caught up in looking for *the* right answer or *the* right choice God wants made. In this workbook we will use the phrases "God's yearning" or "God's longing" because they suggest a larger number of life choices and indicate a more interactive relationship with the God who calls individuals and organizations into future possibilities. Jeremiah 29:11-14 reminds us that God does have plans for us. We are encouraged to seek God's vision because it is multifaceted and brings hope, no matter the circumstances. Encouragement to listen to God's longing is a more open context for examining the issues or questions before the corporate body.

What Is Discernment?

Most people ask, *How do we know what God wants us to do?* and *How do we know when God is speaking and it is not our voice echoing our own desires?* Spiritual discernment is about finding God's yearning for the direction to live, not a once-and-for-all answer to all questions. When we engage in spiritual discernment, we continually seek to know God's longing and to accept the invitation to live into the abundance and life God so freely offers.

Paying attention to the process of discerning God's desire for a church or organization initiates a journey down paths that lead to a deeper, richer, fuller existence. Discernment involves listening to God, walking in God's way, and choosing life and abundance (see Deut. 30:19). Sometimes churches and organizations do make a choice for death when decisions lead toward divisions in the church family or toward closing down options for growth. Death choices foster fear and desperation. Life choices bring the opposite results. They foster an opening up of relationships that lead toward healing and spiritual growth, that examine new alternatives in the church's life.

The vision in Isaiah 43:18-21 illuminates the discernment process:

> Do not remember the former things
>   or consider the things of old.
> I am about to do a new thing;
>   now it springs forth, do you not perceive it?
> I will make a way in the wilderness
>   and rivers in the desert.
> The wild animals will honor me,
>   the jackals and the ostriches;
> for I give water in the wilderness,
>   rivers in the desert,
> to give drink to my chosen people,
>   the people whom I formed for myself
> so that they might declare my praise.

When churches enter a discernment process, they begin to tap into the water in the desert and can open their eyes to the "new thing" God is doing for them. Discernment allows forgetting and even the healing the "things of old," while at the same time opening up avenues to live out God's vision for ministry and mission.

It is important to understand that God's vision is broad and deep. The new thing God is doing in the church is bigger than anyone could ever imagine. Therefore, the church is not seeking the "right" answer, because there are often several ways to move toward God's vision.

Spiritual discernment is not a new process; it is an ancient practice with roots in the biblical text. Most of the stories of discernment in the Bible are partial stories. The entirety of the journey individuals and the early church embarked upon are not heard. Nevertheless, these stories offer clues to various parts of discernment. Throughout this workbook biblical references will help the church understand the discernment process. Take the time to open your Bibles and read the passage in context each time you come upon a biblical reference.

The Process of Discernment

Discernment is a process. It is not linear movement up a ladder, touching each rung while working to get to the right decision. Discernment more closely resembles a dance. Picture two dancers. They move back and forth and across the dance floor. If we could track their movement, we would see that the dancers eventually cover the entire floor, while touching several places more than once. The process of discernment takes us back and forth through many activities, touching some places more than once.

Our vision of discernment is described in the diagram on page 19. God is in the center of the diagram connecting all the circles that represent components of the process. These circles are surrounded by a large ring signifying the mission of the church or organization. Between the circles are spaces that make up the foundational pieces of covenant (see chapter 2) and worshipful-work (see chapter 3). The process moves into the various circles; God is always at the center of the movement from circle to circle, reminding us that community building and worship act as foundations for seeking God's yearning for our mission.

The movement of discernment enters each circle. If a circle is skipped, eventually the movement comes back to it. The circular design of the diagram

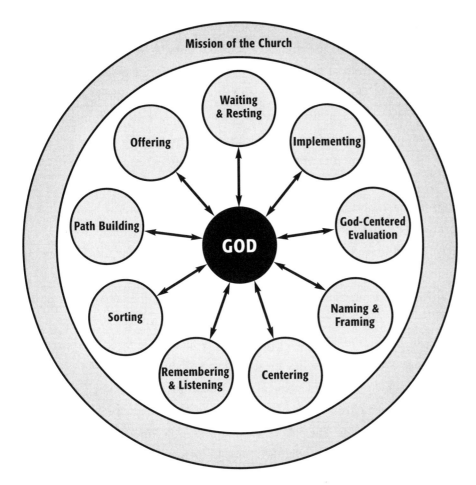

The Movements in Discernment

acknowledges what is often true: a group will keep coming back to the same spot. Yet, each time that circle is entered, the examination of the issue goes a little deeper, and the group can heal and let go of the disturbances that bind them at that point. Returning to issues at a new level of discussion allows for increased clarity and a deeper engagement in discerning God's longing for the church.

How Does the Discernment Process Begin?

How does a faith community move intentionally into the future while listening to God's leading? The first step is to gather a group of leaders who covenant together to put the time and energy into becoming the discernment team for the church. Why? Because shifts in a church's identity and mission do happen when a small group of dedicated people learn to practice prayer and discernment together. This group's growth and experiences of becoming a supportive community lead the individual members to articulate the meanings and values they are discovering for the entire congregation.

The discernment team may be the church board/council/session/long-range planning committee, or a group of mature Christians willing to enter into this sacred process. Each potential team member should spend time in prayer and reflection in order to see if God is calling him or her to be on the team. In addition, everyone needs to be willing to spend the time required in individual and corporate prayer for the meetings of the team. Discernment team members must also be willing to listen to one another and to the congregation. While each person is charged with listening to God, each one is also charged with attending to all the avenues in which the Holy Spirit moves.

No one person holds all the wisdom, but everyone holds part of the wisdom.

Every church approaches spiritual discernment from its own direction, because each church has developed a particular personality type (see chapter 3). Individuals within each church also come to this spiritual activity with varying backgrounds. The people within the church come to the process with mixed levels of self-awareness and different degrees of comfort with various approaches to decision making and styles of handling challenges. They come with a range of experience in their relationship with and knowledge of God. God will speak to each church in a variety of venues with different messages, and individuals will hear God in just as many ways.

In corporate spiritual discernment, a group enters the process in order to discern God's yearning for the whole ministry. No one person can discern for the group; rather it takes the collective listening and wisdom of the entire discernment team to hear God's yearning. Mary Benet McKinney says no one person holds all the wisdom, but everyone holds part of the wisdom.[3] In other words, when team members come to the meetings, they share what they have been hearing from the Holy Spirit. Each person holds part of the message, and the entire group moves closer to God's yearning when each person can share what he or she has heard. Joint wisdom is greater than the wisdom of any one person. Listening to one another is the key to the corporate discernment process. (See chapter 5 for more information on attentive listening skills.)

Plan for broad communication with the entire church as an essential component of the discernment process. The church will ease into its new future based on God's yearning if members have been kept up to date. The discernment team can keep the congregation posted on what they have discovered through newsletters, announcements on Sunday morning, and by visiting various groups in the church.

The Church of the Future

Although many churches are living in patterns that worked successfully in the past, these patterns do not draw the church into the future. Church people can no longer operate with past models, expecting that life together will be familiar and safe. Most have begun to realize that business as usual is leading to the end of an era in church life. Today leaders are being called to prepare for the church of the future, into which the Spirit is breathing new life and stretching boundaries.

The shape of the future church is not yet clear. Nor is the future of today's churches. However, new church forms keep popping up in unlikely places. What is clear is the call to engage in the basic practices of spiritual formation as the new patterns for the larger Christian community are being revealed.

Diana Butler Bass in *The Practicing Congregation: Imagining a New Old Church* presents the idea that new vibrant churches are not based on the latest ideas but rather are engaged in intentionality, genuine community, ancient spiritual practices, discernment, and storytelling, among other things. The church is moving into a place where faith is authentic. Genuine spirituality draws people to churches.

CHAPTER TWO

Discernment Team Foundation

Scripture: *Psalm 25:8-10*

Good and upright is the Lord;
    therefore he instructs sinners in the way.
He leads the humble in what is right,
    and teaches the humble his way.
All the paths of the Lord are steadfast love and faithfulness,
    for those who keep his covenant and his decrees.

Introduction

AS THE PROCESS begins, the discernment team can focus on three activities:

- discussing the group's identity and its mission;
- drawing up a covenant with one another;
- building community by getting to know one another better.

Group formation and community building are essential for the discernment process. Building trust and practicing attentive listening will enhance a group's time together. Working in a small group succeeds when participants know the people beside them and across the room. The tasks seem easier and move more quickly when people trust that the others at the table have prayed about their joint work. Defensive behavior and energy devoted to "my" point dissipate when the people sitting around the table know each other and are truly listening.

Focus of the Group Mission

Begin the group interaction with some questions about why people have come together. Then ask, *With what task is the group charged?* For example:

- Selecting church leaders
- Selecting a pastor
- Developing a vision for the church
- Evaluation and strategic planning
- Other

Take time for this discussion because the group cannot assume everyone knows and understands the task or mission.

> We worked with a group of people from several churches who struggled through their first two meetings. Even though they enjoyed getting to know one another and were doing some good work, there was an underlying tension and struggle. It became evident that they weren't clear as to their mission. They had different views on the reasons they had been called together. We took time for them to tell the story of why they had been formed and what their task was as a group. Telling the story of their formation not only cleared up misunderstandings; it also filled in some gaps. Some people had been struggling because they didn't have all of the information about their call. As soon as everyone was on the same page, the work became easier. People no longer had to spend energy trying to understand who they were.

Developing a Covenant

Turning the individuals who have gathered for their joint task into a "we" of community is one of the first things to do. "Establishing a clear covenant empowers each person in the group."[1] A covenant concerns how to work together and how to behave when the members of the group are apart. The discerning community, no matter the reason for gathering, needs to develop a covenant.

The covenant is a way to honor the gifts each person brings to the community's work. Each person brings life experiences and wisdom. Learning to celebrate the uniqueness of each person, especially when the group begins to feel the differences among members, helps to celebrate the gifts and to tolerate the idiosyncrasies of each person.

The purpose of the covenant is to address matters of confidentiality and the ways the group will be with each other during its work. The covenant commits each member of the group to listen carefully to the others. The covenant also includes a commitment to the patience and prayer needed in the process of spiritual discernment as the group seeks ways to place God in the center of their life together.

Each discernment team will develop its own covenant based on its mission and the individuals involved. The covenant will also lift up and give focus to the commitment required of everyone. Use the following list of topics as a starting point. Type up the covenant and distribute among the members of the team.

Covenant Topics to Consider
On newsprint record the team's thoughts in the following areas:

How will we be with each other during our work?
- Confidentiality
- Honesty
- Attentiveness
- Attendance
- Listening to one another
- Respect
- Other

How will we be with God?
- Commitment to join in prayer
    - ~during meetings
    - ~between meetings
- Commitment to engage scripture
- Commitment to reflect on the historic witness of our faith community
- Commitment to seek and express God's longing
- Commitment to listen to God first
- Corporate confession regarding
    - ~personal agendas
    - ~fears
    - ~taking control
- Thanksgiving for opportunities to grow

During the first meeting of the group, besides bringing clarity to the mission, include time to develop this covenant. After the meeting, one member can type a draft and distribute it for everyone's review. If additional discussion on the covenant is needed, that can continue at the second meeting. Patterns of working together are best set at the beginning, and a covenant establishes an agreed upon way of doing God's business together.

The covenant is a commitment to one another that binds the group together. In the covenant the group decides ahead of time how to handle group interactions. The process of discernment comes more easily when the group members trust one another and know they are committed to the same way of being. Struggles will still arise as the group works together, and yet members will meet the challenges more easily with a covenant in place.

Building a Sense of Community

Getting to know one another is a core piece of the discernment process and essential to any committee's work (see chapter 3). When the group first gathers, emphasizing that you "recognize that the basis of life together is not personal affinity but the grace of God" sets the foundational understanding for the life of the group.[2] Listening to one another's faith story fosters an understanding of the perspectives and origins of each individual's faith journey. Appreciating the individual differences makes it harder to show disrespect toward another person in the group. Learning how God has worked in the life of the individuals around the table begins to enable recognition that God is present at the table. The practice of listening to each other at deep levels means each one practices listening for God.

What are the ways to tell faith stories? There are several methods, but the following ones can launch the process of faith-story sharing. Remember to designate a leader for each exercise (see page 13).

Sharing Faith Stories

Each person will be asked to share part of his or her holy story by answering one of the following questions:

- When have you sensed God as a companion on your journey?
- When have you sensed God was in the midst of a major decision you made?

First create sacred space by arranging the chairs in a circle. (Do not sit around a table.) Light a candle to represent Christ's presence.

Sharing and receiving the stories

- Sit in silence and allow the Holy Spirit to move a member of the group to share.
- The individual shares his/her answer to one of the questions above in five to seven minutes.
- When the person is finished, say thank you and remain in silence.
- Silently lift the person up in prayer, thanking God for the person's life and asking God to bless him or her. Do not voice specific prayer requests for the person, but simply hold the individual in God's loving presence.
- Sit in silence until another person feels moved to share.
- When everyone has shared, say a prayer of thanksgiving for everyone's holy story.
- The size of the group may necessitate sharing the stories over two meetings or in a one-day retreat.

Silence after each story honors the person and reinforces the practice of holy listening. When the only vocal response to a person's sharing is "thank you," everyone moves toward a deeper listening. Shifting quickly to another's story would promote shallow listening, because the next person is formulating remarks rather than savoring the story just told. Deep listening allows hearing the content of one another's faith journey. Learning to listen to each other begins to move the whole group toward an atmosphere of discernment.

Continue to ask God to bless your interactions within the group. The discernment team members will be spending a lot of time together while they seek God's yearning for their church or organization. The process of getting to know one another and agreeing on how to work together lays a foundation for this work. Building community now also means members look forward to time spent together.

CHAPTER THREE

Developing an Atmosphere for Discernment

SCRIPTURE: *Deuteronomy 1:13-14*

[And Moses said to the congregation:] "Choose for each of your tribes individuals who are wise, *discerning*, and reputable to be your leaders." [The community answered him,] "The plan you have proposed is a good one." (emphasis added)

Introduction

DISCERNMENT takes preparation. Before a church or organization enters into the process, it is important to develop an atmosphere for discernment. Gardening requires preparation of the soil before planting the seeds. Cooking requires gathering the ingredients before putting them together to make the dish. A business presentation requires pulling together materials for a PowerPoint or a planning outline. In order to listen to God and to sense the movement of the Holy Spirit in the discernment process, an atmosphere where God's voice can be heard is essential. This chapter explores ways the discernment team and the church can prepare themselves to live into God's yearning for their life and mission.

Current Systems of Management

One major consideration in creating an atmosphere conducive to discernment is a church's approach to meetings and decision-making systems. The church often conducts meetings in the same manner as a corporation or other business organization. The church modifies the business model by adding prayer to the beginning and end of the meeting, but most often that is the only difference.

Decision-making and planning structures in churches do vary, and yet they usually rely on *Robert's Rules of Order* and parliamentary procedure for the orderly conduct of business. These tried-and-true methods have been effective in meetings over the years. However, the structure becomes the authority for the conduct of business. The Holy Spirit can move, but human-made procedures put limitations on that movement. Parker Palmer says, "Democracy is the only place where 51 percent of the people can tell 49 percent of the people they are wrong."[1] Parliamentary procedures set up an atmosphere of win-lose and the need for each party to defend its own position.

Over the years churches have used many systems for planning and management of time and resources: management by objective; strategic-planning methods; development of goals and objectives, and so on. These methods rely on plans for the future, evaluation of progress, and measurable outcomes. They reflect the value of the bottom line and are often numbers-driven. They tend to be oriented toward measuring success quantitatively rather than qualitatively. Again, the Holy Spirit is able to work within these business systems. However, when management heads in these directions, the planners typically decide in advance what achieving success looks like, and then ask God to bless that success. The planning teams set the bottom line based on numbers rather than being focused on doing God's mission in this world. The center of achievement is goal-based rather than God-based.

Take time to consider the specific methods currently used to conduct business in your church:

Current Systems

How do you currently conduct business and make decisions in the committees and leadership circles of your church? (*Robert's Rules of Order*, planning by objective, etc.)

What kind of atmosphere does this system establish?

How do you know God's presence is in the meetings?

How do you feel when you leave meetings?

The methods for conducting meetings and establishing goals for churches *typically* lead to struggles between opposing viewpoints and forced compromises. There is another way that can bring a new energy to church meetings; that way emerges from a biblical foundation and places God in the center of the meeting and planning sessions.

Biblical Basis for Meetings

In chapter 1 we talked about Christ as the head of the church. If everything a church accomplishes is God's business, then God should be in the middle of the business. Biblical evidence—and directions—confirm that a faith-based way of doing church business is both traditional and effective. What does scripture have to say about how to approach meetings in the church? Two important passages speak to this context: 1 Corinthians 12:12-31 and Romans 12:1-2.

The apostle Paul in his letters to the church at Corinth focuses on issues of leadership and the spiritual gifts that strengthen the fellowship of believers. Here in chapter 12 of 1 Corinthians, Paul uses the metaphor of the human body to image ways the spiritual gifts function to enhance the entire church. Verse 27 reminds us that we are one body: "Now you are the body of Christ and individually members of it." We come together as the body of Christ in our business as well as in worship and programming activities. Because the community of faith is one body, each person involved is a part of that body with gifts and skills that strengthen the whole community. Christ is the head, and the business of the church can be conducted accordingly with Christ in the lead.

Chuck Olsen looks to another text, Romans 12:1-2, as the foundation for an understanding of worshipful-work, the method for integrating spirituality and business.[2]

> I appeal to you therefore, brothers and sisters, by the mercies of God, to present your bodies as a living sacrifice, holy and acceptable to God, which is your spiritual worship. Do not be conformed to this world, but be transformed by the renewing of your minds, so that you may discern what is the will of God—what is good and acceptable and perfect.

The atmosphere of discernment arises out of these verses. When a board or a committee gathers, individuals bring their own spirituality into the meetings. However, at the threshold of the room, a transformation can take place. Their individual spirituality becomes a corporate spirituality. That community of people is called to let go, to relinquish their own idea of what that board or committee ought to be, and to approach the business of the church in a new way.

> I appeal to you . . . to present your bodies as a living sacrifice.

The biblical language of sacrifice carries a tactile dimension. People presented the first fruits of the harvest and the firstborn of the animals to the Lord and relinquished them. The sacrificial offering was prepared by human hands and then released. Letting go, relinquishing, and releasing are difficult but necessary activities.

To present and let go of an animal for sacrifice is hard. To present and let go of ourselves and our assumptions is also hard. All the various methods for achieving an effective board are relinquished when you move into the sacrificial space of the discerning board or committee.

Paul uses the Greek word *soma,* translated "bodies," which refers to the entire body, or whole being. Each individual person is to present his or her entire being—everything he or she is—to God. Taking this a step further, if the gathered community is the body of Christ, then that community lets go of itself in order to belong to God. Like individuals, the community is asked to present all that it is and all that it does to God.

Chuck Olsen has introduced an interesting aspect to this scripture by replacing the word *bodies* with *meetings*: present your meetings as a living sacrifice. Meetings, the work the community does together, *are* to be presented to God. The room in which the meeting takes place becomes sacred space, and the meeting itself becomes the sacrifice—that offering that is lifted up, let go of, and dedicated to God.

Invite release by beginning a meeting with Communion. The refocusing of the Lord's Supper encourages individuals to re-center in the community. The leader can ask, "What do the elements mean to us: the bread broken and the wine poured out?" The conversation and reflection on the meaning of the elements of Communion become the opportunity to observe what the community is holding onto and where prayer supports the actions of letting go. "Prayers of confession, both corporate and individual, both spoken and silent, can deepen the process."[3]

The second verse of Romans 12 adds another dimension.

> Do not be conformed to this world, but be transformed by the renewing of your minds.

The imperative of the Greek word *suschematizo,* meaning to form or mold after something, to be conformed or guided by, points the direction of Paul's dichotomy. The church is not to pattern our ways of business after the ways the world does business. The church should not be co-opting the worldly business patterns but needs to be countercultural in approaching God's business.

The contrast to *suschematizo* is *metamorphoo,* a verb meaning to change or to transform, which corresponds to the English word *metamorphosis*. When a caterpillar is turning into a butterfly, there is one point in the chrysalis when the mass of cells is neither a caterpillar nor a butterfly. One form changes completely into the other. The church needs metamorphosis into a new way of being, a complete change in the conduct of business.

The phrase "the renewing of your minds" finds Paul using the Greek word *nous,* translated "mind," which means disposition with a nuance toward a mode of thought and the moral core. The Greek word does not imply only the reasoning, thinking part of the mind but also the inner core or the mental side of a person that is feeling, willing, and thinking. The nature of the business meeting, then, becomes renewed and transformed.

> . . . so that you may discern what is the will of God—what is good and acceptable and perfect.

The movement from conformation into transformation prepares the way for discernment. "To discern" in Greek is the verb *dokimazo*, which has a range of meanings: to examine, discern, test, and prove. Used by Paul in Romans, the Corinthian correspondence, Galatians, Philippians, and the first letter to the Thessalonians, the verb suggests being able to sort out thoughts and actions in order to ascertain what is true. Here in Romans, Paul encourages us to test and prove the will (*thelema*—desire, longing, what one wishes to happen) of God. Then Paul gives three qualifiers: what is good (*agathos*—fit, valuable, useful), and what is acceptable (*euarestos*—pleasing, giving satisfaction), and what is perfect (*teleios*—having attained the end or purpose, fully developed).[4]

Paul's appeal challenges the churches to open up their meetings in order to be transformed into discerning communities. The actions of testing, proving, sorting, and listening are the ways to live into becoming valuable, satisfactory, and fully developed churches.

Read aloud in the group the following translation of Romans 12:1-2:

I appeal to you therefore, brothers and sisters, by the mercies of God, to present your meetings as a living sacrifice, holy and acceptable to God, which is your spiritual worship. Do not be conformed to this world, but be totally changed by the renewing of your inner core, so that you may discern what is the longing of God—what is valuable and pleasing and fully developed. (AT)

Use these questions to reflect on the reading:
- How is your understanding of meetings changed with this translation?
- What does it mean to you to present your meetings as a living sacrifice?
- What does it mean to conduct your meetings in a countercultural way?
- What does it mean to you to pray for your meetings to be valuable, pleasing, and fully developed before God?

We can read this passage of scripture as a call to conduct church business in a whole new way. The business becomes spiritual worship. The business of the church changes in nature to be in rhythm with everything the church does. One pastor in a training session we conducted said, "Oh, I see, this is not about strategies; this is about a way of life."

On June 30, 2007, after a season of discernment, the Discerning Overseers of Worshipful-Work® dissolved the organization as a resourcing and programming entity. The legacy of the ministry as well as the trademark Worshipful-Work® were passed on to Water in the Desert Ministries. For more information, visit www.waterinthedesert.org

Worshipful-Work®

The biblical text guides us to an understanding that our business needs to be worshipful. Centering our work on the Trinity enables the leaders of the church to call on the power of God, the presence of Christ, and the wisdom of the Holy Spirit in new ways. The scriptures lead to a new dimension of corporate life where leadership, decision making, planning, and administration become *faith-based*. Chuck Olsen offers a discussion of what he calls "worshipful-work" in *Transforming Church Boards into Communities of Spiritual Leaders*. He has been a pioneer in this area for our day, and his book can be a useful tool for the discernment team.

In a worshipful-work approach, the meetings are conducted as worship. The approach assumes that God is present and active in every church meeting whether it be the governing body, the finance committee, or the mission of the deacons. Gradually the church moves toward a time when worship and the business of the church share more similarities than differences. A church can anticipate that meetings of the various boards and committees will become spiritually renewing experiences rather than mentally exhausting. As one pastor commented after a training session at his church, "Wouldn't it be great if we could say, 'Wow, I just left a finance committee meeting, and it was a spiritually renewing experience'?"

Taking time to listen to God is essential, and that requires training ears and hearts to listen to God in meetings. Watching and listening for God's presence does not come easily. "Only bird watchers can discern the song of oriole or thrush from among a cacophony of sounds. Why? Because their ears are tuned to no other sounds but the singing from the birds."[5] Meetings need to be held at a slower pace in order to hear God. Space for silence during meetings allows for hearing God over the cacophony of our voices.

How can people shift a church's business into a faith-based style of leadership? Begin with spiritual formation. The church boards or committees that transition into worshipful-work most easily are made up of members who have been participating in personal spiritual formation. Spiritual formation deepens the relationship with God. Bringing God into the center of meetings is easier when individuals in the meetings are connected to God in many areas of life.

To initiate an intentional program of spiritual formation in your church, start by using resources like the Companions in Christ series (Upper Room Books) in small groups. Shift meeting agendas into spiritual experiences by reading together *Transforming Church Boards into Communities of Spiritual Leaders* by Charles M. Olsen. Deepen the prayer life of congregational members by using resources like *A Praying Congregation: The Art of Teaching Spiritual Practice* by Jane E. Vennard. Form prayer groups that pray for individuals and for the congregation. Ask people to enter into a time of prayer and Bible study every day. Each of these actions builds a foundation for worshipful-work.

The structure of a congregation's worship service can serve as an outline for business meetings.[6] Lighting a candle placed at the center of the table reminds people that Christ is present and the center of the meeting. The call to worship focuses the meeting time, and the offering can be the reports presented. Scripture reading provides a foundation, and a hymn expresses a time of celebration for the meeting. The content of the business items becomes the proclamation of the Word for the governing group. Prayer can surround all these elements. Closing with a benediction completes the meeting time.

The business of the church should be undergirded with corporate prayer. Here are some methods of encouraging that support: (1) Distribute a list of meeting dates and times to individuals who agree to be prayer partners for various committees or boards. They can pray before and during the time of meetings. (2) Invite committee members to lift up fellow members in prayer before everyone gathers for a meeting. (3) Slow down the pace of meetings, making space for prayer and silence that allows God's voice to be heard through the voices of the committee members.

In addition to prayer, biblical reflection during meetings can ground the discussion on a solid foundation. Sometimes when a committee gets stuck in a conversation, it is helpful to turn to the stories in the Bible for guidance.

> As we facilitated a discernment process for a group, we asked this question: *If Jesus were doing this work, what would it look like?* The group discussed the question, and one member finally asked, *But how do we go about doing the work?* The group turned to the Bible for guidance. They found the story of Jesus sending out the seventy in Luke 10:1-20. After reflecting on the story, they realized the Luke story gave them a pattern for relating their vision to others.

Appendix A provides additional ideas for introducing an atmosphere of worship in meetings. Often people ask this legitimate question: "Our meetings are long enough; how can we add things to our agenda like biblical reflection, more prayer, faith sharing?" Consider the following comments from people who have started doing business in this new way.

"Our meetings are now shorter since we started spending more time in prayer at the beginning."

"People on my Session [governing board] used to argue with each other all the time. When we started lighting a Christ candle and inviting God into all that we do, the arguing stopped. Now we listen closely to each other and recognize the Christ in each other. We still have our differences, but now we listen for God's voice and have stopped trying to defend our own voices."

"Finding a biblical story that gave us a paradigm for the issue we were facing meant we didn't have to discuss the item forever."

It is not necessary to change everything at once. Preaching or offering a Bible study on Romans 12:1-2 can set the stage for change. One church found it helpful to initiate the changes in their staff meetings first. When introducing the changes, ease into this new way of doing business. Worshipful-work can make a difference.

Who Are We As a Discernment Team?

Just as people have individual personalities that affect their decision making, so do boards and committees, and even churches. Each personality type will have strengths and weaknesses. Knowing the ways various personality types approach decisions will make committee members alert to those differences during meetings. Working together means taking into account how each person processes information.

There are several ways to explore personality types. Many people are familiar with the Myers-Briggs personality type indicators. The questions and types developed by Isabel Briggs Myers and Katharine Cook Briggs found in their personality studies are widely used in church circles and across denominations. Each person operates mainly out of one perspective in each of the four pairs of preferences.

If you are not familiar with the Myers-Briggs Types, you may explore the types online at www.personalitypathways.com/type or conduct an Internet search for "Myers-Briggs Types" to locate many Web sites. There is also a simplified test, the Keirsey Temperament Sorter, in David Keirsey and Marilyn Bates, *Please Understand Me: Character and Temperament Types*, 5–10.

Another personality inventory, the Enneagram, can be used fruitfully when exploring foundational assumptions. The Enneagram is based on nine fundamental personality types and their complex relationships. This tool has its roots in spiritual wisdom and can be adapted by most religious traditions. For more information on the Enneagram, see *The Wisdom of the Enneagram* by Don Riso and Russ Hudson. You can take a Enneagram test on their Web site: www.enneagraminstitute.com. People can learn more about their own personality type and prayer in *The Enneagram and Prayer* by Barbara Metz and John Burchill.

As committees work together, note how each person on the team approaches the decision-making process. For example, the extrovert will want to process all the information verbally in order to come to an understanding of the issue at hand. The introvert will need silence and space to process the information. Often he or she will need to be invited to speak. The sensing person will want all the facts before making a decision. The intuitive person will tend to leap ahead and may miss some important pieces. The thinking person will tend to stay logical and have some difficulty listening for the stirrings of the Holy Spirit. The feeling person may have a challenge in separating his or her interior feelings from the voices of other people. Finally, the perceiving person will have a hard time bringing the process to a close, because there may be one more possibility to explore. As you work together, you will discover the different personality types in one another. Identifying the strengths and challenges of each type and celebrating the variations can help the team function more effectively.

Each congregation has its strengths and weaknesses and shares the love of Christ with others in its own way. Typically people are drawn to churches and organizations that match or complement their individual personality type. And yet, individuals "need one another as complementary members of the body of Christ."[7] We have found two good methods of exploring a church's personality. Corinne Ware in *Discover Your Spiritual Type: A Guide to Individual and Congregational Growth* offers one based on how church members go about knowing and conceptualizing God.[8] The book provides a questionnaire for church members that points to their own spirituality types and then to their congregational spiritual type. It is well worth the time to take this questionnaire as a congregation, or at least as a committee.

Celia Hahn offers a creative way of looking at a church body.[9] She suggests drawing a person on a large piece of newsprint and asking: "Who is this person, (*Name of Church*)?"

The Church As a Person
- Draw an outline of a person on a large piece of newsprint.
- Put the name of the church at the top of the newsprint.
- Ask the following questions, recording the answers on the newsprint. Write and draw the answers on the person-outline as is appropriate:

    If this person is _____:
    (Name of Church)

    What does this person look like?
    What gifts does this person have?

What weaknesses does this person have?

How does this person relate to God?

How does this person play?

How does this person handle stress and conflict?

How does this person process information?

How old does this person act?

What gender is this person?

How does God see this person?

- Stand back and see what new information you have discovered.

This personal identity exercise uses the congregation's knowledge of itself to construct a metaphor, a dynamic model of the congregation as a person. Janet Cawley describes the result of one such exercise with the South Valley Church. The church is in a fast-growing new suburb and is only ten years old. Most families in the church have young children, and both parents are working. Time and money are limited, but generous giving means the budget is met and the mortgage is being paid down. People have different ideas as to what should happen next. Janet describes their experience when a consultant led them through the church-as-a-person exercise.

Then the consultant asked them to try to imagine what kind of body South Valley was. After all, bodies come in all shapes and sizes, all races and social conditions and states of health. So, if they had to imagine South Valley as a particular body, what would that person be like? Which gender, about how old, what occupation, what state of health and fitness? What would be the life challenges and dilemmas of such a person?

They broke into their table groups and began to discuss this interesting question. There was lots of laughter and energy and when the consultant called them back, it seemed too soon. Surprisingly, they had all come up with basically the same image. They agreed that South Valley was sort of like a teenaged boy, about thirteen years old.

- boundless energy, but could fall asleep for long periods
- great enthusiasm, but not such great organization
- terrific at short-term projects, but easily bored if anything went on too long
- growing out of his pants every few months

- voice wobbling up and down
- wide-eyed and open hearted

Everyone laughed in recognition, and they had all come up with the same image! Maybe they were onto something! They decided to call this wonderful person Eddie.[10]

The consultant went on to ask what Eddie needed in order to flourish and what it means for their future if the church is a thirteen-year-old boy.

Self-knowledge is valuable for both individuals and congregations. Tracing how the identity of the church "person" matures over time (through the functioning of its committees and in its business) and watching for new ways this "person" grows can inform the discernment process. One important question is: *How does this person relate to God?* The images for God that are held by individuals and the committees of the church influence the atmosphere for discernment. Images for God affect relationships with God.

Who Is God?

People bring sets of presuppositions to church business regarding their understanding of how God interacts with the community of faith and with them as individuals. Individuals have been taught to "see" God in particular ways, especially those who grew up in the church. The images and assumptions about God's person and actions may have shifted over the years, or the first image for God learned as a child may still be primary. Understanding who God is affects faith development and relationship with the Trinity. Understanding how God interacts with humankind will make a difference in understanding our worshipful-work and the discernment process.

There is a thorough discussion of personal images for God in our workbook *Living into the Answers: A Workbook for Personal Spiritual Discernment.* The exercises in chapter 2 of *Living into the Answers* explore personal images for God. Those exercises are reproduced in appendix B of this workbook. You may wish to work through those before focusing on a corporate understanding of the images for God.

The following discussion will concentrate on the ways the community images God and how these affect its process of discernment. The questions to be answered when thinking about corporate images for God include: *Who is the God we invite into our meetings? Is God intimately connected with our business, or does God leave us to do our work and make our decisions on our own?*

Identify your discernment team's primary images for God.

How would you describe the God to whom you pray?

Are the images of God different when you are in trouble?

How would you describe God in worship settings?

Is one of the primary images for the God of the committee a transcendent God sitting on a throne, high and lifted up?

In the year that King Uzziah died, I saw the Lord sitting on a throne, high and lofty; and the hem of his robe filled the temple. Seraphs were in attendance above him; each had six wings: with two they covered their faces, and with two they covered their feet, and with two they flew. And one called to another and said:
"Holy, holy, holy is the Lord of hosts;
the whole earth is full of his glory." (ISAIAH 6:1-3)

Or perhaps the group received its images for the transcendent God from Ezekiel 1:26-28 or Revelation 4. In these texts God is enthroned and controls both nature and history.

Is the God who comes to church meetings the One who created humankind in God's image?

Then God said, "Let us make humankind ['*adam*] in our image, according to our likeness; and let them have dominion over the fish of the sea, and over the birds of the air, and over the cattle, and over all the wild animals of the earth, and over every creeping thing that creeps upon the earth."

So God created humankind ['adam] in his image,
in the image of God he created them;
male and female he created them.

God blessed them, and God said to them, "Be fruitful and multiply, and fill the earth and subdue it; and have dominion over the fish of the sea and over the birds of the air and over every living thing that moves upon the earth." (GENESIS 1:26-28)

Or—

Then the Lord God formed man ['adam] from the dust of the ground ['adamah], and breathed into his nostrils the breath of life. (GENESIS 2:7)

Psalm 139:7-10 presents a picture of God who is everywhere:

Where can I go from your spirit?
Or where can I flee from your presence?
If I ascend to heaven, you are there;
if I make my bed in Sheol, you are there.
If I take the wings of the morning
and settle at the farthest limits of the sea,
even there your hand shall lead me,
and your right hand shall hold me fast.

John 1:1-5 connects with Genesis 1 in the actions of word and creation:

In the beginning was the Word, and the Word was with God, and the Word was God. He was in the beginning with God. All things came into being through him, and without him not one thing came into being. What has come into being in him was life, and the life was the light of all people. The light shines in the darkness, and the darkness did not overcome it.

The Bible presents multiple images for God and the ways God is present in the community of faith. *Which of these images is the main one the committee relies on when people enter a business meeting or embark on the discernment process?* Perhaps the image for God people bring into a meeting is not a biblical image at all but one that has evolved over time within the community. If God is disconnected or even transcendent without the corresponding immanence, it is difficult to follow a path of trust and assurance of God's interest in the faith-based discernment process.

Groups who discuss their corporate images for God often say, *Of course, God cares about our meetings.* Yet, when they begin doing the exercises on the following pages, they realize they can affirm that God is present and cares about the meeting, but spiritually and emotionally they don't bring that understanding into the meeting itself. Somehow they leave the intimate, personal, caring images for God at the door when a church committee meeting begins.

As participants in corporate worship, we often gather up a variety of images for God from the hymns, anthems, and choruses we sing through the church year. Music used in worship or heard on Christian radio provides a good source for discussion of people's favorite images for God and their experience of God in worship and daily life.

The next exercises encourage participants to uncover the images for God they bring with them. The exercises are not easy. They are divided into two sections because of the length of time needed to complete them. Each exercise requires a minimum of two hours. Both can be completed in one all-day retreat.

Corporate Images for God—Part 1
Music
Preparation
Gather examples of images for God in the hymns and choruses your church likes to sing. Pick out the stanzas or lines that describe God. Design a handout with these selections printed on it.

Exercise
- Give everyone the prepared handout.
- Sing the selections on the sheet.
- Talk about the images for God in the songs, recording what is said on newsprint.
- Ask people to consider which image for God guides them in daily life.
- Allow a few minutes of silence for reflection.
- Share your reflections, recording them on newsprint.
- Ask each person to consider which image for God guides them in meetings.
- Allow a few minutes of silence for reflection.
- Share your reflections, recording them on newsprint.
- What are the differences and similarities between people's perception of God in a personal context and God in the context of a group meeting?

Scripture
Read the following scripture passages aloud for the group:

> Isaiah 6:1-3
> Revelation 4
> Genesis 1:26-28 and 2:7
> Psalm 139:7-10
> John 1:1-5

- After each scripture passage is read, discuss the image (or images) for God in the passage, recording the comments on newsprint.
- Ask the same questions listed above under "Music."

Comparing the imagery presented by music and scripture helps people clarify their assumptions about God's activities. The second exercise builds upon this comparison and asks for deeper reflection.

Corporate Images for God—Part 2
Meetings
- Post the images for God discussed in the previous exercise.
- Give everyone the handouts typed up after the last meeting (on images for God in scripture and music and which images guide them personally and in meetings).
- Give everyone time to look over these summaries.
- Look at the list of images individuals identified as guides in daily life.
- Are there images that appear often on many lists?

- Look at the list of images people identified as guides in meetings.
- Are there images that appear often here?
- What are the differences and similarities in the two lists?
- If there is a difference between images of God related to personal life and images of God related to corporate life, discuss why this may be the case.
     For example, if God is a personal God in daily life, why then is God not a personal God in meetings? Do people leave God at the door when they go into church meetings?
- How can the group learn to bring God into meetings based on how individuals relate to God in their daily lives?
- Read Psalm 139:7-10 again, and discuss the following questions:
     Can we hide from God?
     Where is God?
     Can we hide from God in meetings?
     Is God in our meetings?
- Read Romans 12:1-2 again and discuss the following questions:
     What does the scripture say regarding God's will?
     If Christians are to discern God's will, then is God an active player in meetings?
- Based on these exercises, what image of God is helpful to bring into meetings?
- Discuss how these different images for God affect meetings:
     God seated on a throne (Isaiah 6)
     God as a warrior with a strong right arm (Exodus 15)
     God as a shepherd (Isaiah 40 and John 10)
     God as a trickster or a clockmaker

Closing Prayer
Creator and loving God who walks with us, remind us that you care about all we do. Remind us that you are just as interested in what we do in our meetings as you are interested in our individual lives. Help us to find ways to encounter you in our corporate business. Help us to acknowledge your presence. In Christ's name, Amen.

In summary, take time to discuss music imagery and scripture passages that remind us God is relational and connected to the community of faith. God walks with us (Emmanuel) and calls upon us to listen for God's yearning (Jer. 25). We cannot hide from God in our meetings (Ps. 139). By exploring these affirmations about God's actions people can better identify their beliefs about the many ways God is present in their lives and church activities.

God's Love for Us

The team has now examined images for God and has found a variety of ways God is in relationship with individuals and the church. The fundamental image, however, is that God is love. In an article for the journal *Weavings*, Wendy Wright describes hearing a sermon on Jesus' baptism and his time in the wilderness, a time in which he must discern the spirits. The preacher spoke of the words Jesus heard at his baptism: *This is my Son, the Beloved, with whom I am well pleased* (Matt. 3:17). Before Jesus entered the wilderness and a time of discernment, he was claimed as a child of God and told he was loved.[11]

We shared this passage through an exercise called *lectio divina* (see appendix C) with a church discernment team. We asked participants to think of their church as they listened to the biblical story of Jesus' baptism, and we then discussed what people heard. One man spoke up and said, "Wow, this means God loves us and is pleased with us even before we do anything as a church. That is a very freeing and comforting place to be in."

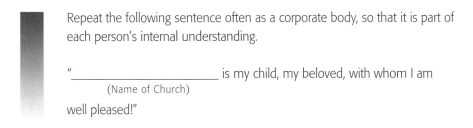

Repeat the following sentence often as a corporate body, so that it is part of each person's internal understanding.

"_____ is my child, my beloved, with whom I am
        (Name of Church)
well pleased!"

Mystery of God

Another critical element in developing an atmosphere for discernment is recognizing that God is mystery. Author Steve Doughty tells about an experience at a conference. After several days of note taking and storytelling, participants climbed a hill for worship. During that worship time, the Spirit of God moved and touched them deeply. Back in their meeting room, the conference leader said, "You've all trained your minds well. Don't ever lose that. But if you want renewal in your faith communities, you've got to recover your sense of mystery."

Steve goes on to talk about the mystery of God and our corporate lives. He offers the following question for consideration: *Where have we experienced the divine mystery in our common life?* Steve catches an important piece of the discussion on images for God and the discernment process. In order to prepare for discernment, ask yourselves where your corporate life has been touched by the mystery of God. Telling those stories of God's timing and of God's presence will undergird the larger discussion in discernment.[12]

Discuss the question: *Where have we experienced the divine mystery in our common life?*

Note the places in your own life where you have experienced God's timing as different from your own. Or share the stories of times when you have felt God's presence. What do these stories tell the members of the group about how we experience God?

Remember that your group process is part of your worshipful-work and corporate discernment. Continue to pay attention to what the group is hearing from God. Note the ways that the group is inviting God into its work. For those who are comfortable with journals, the discipline of journaling is a good spiritual practice. Encourage the many ways that each member of the group can record personal thoughts for sharing at the next meeting or can process feelings about the discernment process as it proceeds.

CHAPTER FOUR

Naming and Framing

Introduction

VISIONING AND PLANNING aren't easy, especially when churches face crucial decisions concerning the life of the organization. This circle in the discernment process addresses the ways a church or organization can approach decisions and planning from a new perspective. Begin with a sincere desire to include God in decision-making efforts, to listen for divine direction, and to find God's longing for ministry and mission.

Naming the Issues

The first component of this circle in the process is naming the issue that calls for decisions. It may be a crisis, a sense that the church has reached a crossroad, or a nudging from God to shift the church's corporate life and identity. Whatever has come up, there are decisions to be made and issues to resolve. By clearly naming the issues the team takes the first step toward identifying future possibilities.

The way of discernment starts with prayer. Because it is often difficult to sort the voices that come from many directions, ask for God's active presence in the midst of listening. Discernment is a gift of God and is surrounded by grace. When churches enter the process without praying for and seeking God's guidance, they attempt to keep the control themselves, and may be trying to protect themselves from going where God might lead. The following prayer suggestions place divine guidance in the center of decision-making processes. Light a Christ candle or a Trinity candle (candle with three wicks) at the beginning

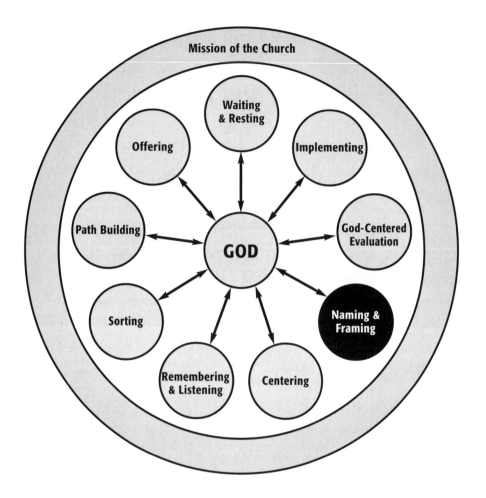

Mission of the Church

Waiting & Resting

Offering

Implementing

Path Building

GOD

God-Centered Evaluation

Sorting

Naming & Framing

Remembering & Listening

Centering

of each meeting. The candle symbolizes Christ's presence within the decision making and serves as a reminder that the work of discernment is about God. Ask for God's power to undergird the work, Jesus' light to shine on the work, and the wisdom of the Holy Spirit to guide the work.

Begin with Prayer:
At the beginning of all gatherings, the discernment team stops to pray, turning the issues and the decisions over to God. Ask for the wisdom of the Holy Spirit to guide the team and for the peace of Christ that surpasses all understandings to surround the team.

Individual

Invite each member of the team to write a prayer for his or her own support and come back to it often as a reminder that no one is alone in this process. The church body and the Trinity are constant companions as each person seeks to discern God's longing for the church.

Corporate

Write a prayer as a team that can be posted at meetings. Start each meeting with the prayer and return to it often. The prayer will remind the team that it does not have the burden of envisioning the church's future alone. The Trinity provides power, companionship, and guidance.

Prayer Support

Invite specific individuals beyond the discernment team, and even outside the church, to pray for the team during the journey of discernment.

Once the process is surrounded by prayer, you can begin to lift up the issues and challenges that are before the church. In order to name the issues that stand before and within a church, first describe the current situation. Explore the reasons for entering the discernment process, talking about the current strengths and challenges in the church, while describing corporate identity (with reference to "the person" of the church you named earlier). These areas for exploration will clarify the issues and establish a starting point for discernment.

Naming and Describing the Issues

- have newsprint, markers, and tape available to record the information
- form small groups to discuss the questions
- bring the ideas back to the large group and record the main issues

Ask the following questions:
Why has the church decided to enter the discernment process?

In light of the church's identity, what are the strengths of this church? In other words, how would people describe the church to others? (Refer to "The Church As a Person" exercise in chapter 3.)

What challenges does the church face?

Group the challenges into categories.
    For example, suppose the following challenges were listed:
        No one wants to be the youth pastor.
        Our youth group is too small for activities.
        Our youth don't attend church.
    All of these could be grouped under one category: Youth

You've spent time listing your strengths and your challenges. The team needs to know what the challenges are, but at this point in the process, the team should not focus on addressing them (developing programs, and so forth). When a church decides to improve weaknesses, they are struggling to fix what they don't have. This focus brings about a sense of inadequacy and makes it hard to feel God's love and to be open to God's vision. As you will see in the next section, often the challenges named are not what God is calling the church to work on. At other times, what appears to be a challenge may actually develop into a strength. It takes the full discernment process to know. Pray about the list and allow God's power to transform it.

Framing the Questions

We live in an "instant" society where people expect quick answers to questions. In the business world we expect overnight delivery. Instant messaging, text messages, and e-mails offer instant communication. No longer do we have to wait several days for a letter to arrive. As a society we have come to expect the answers to today's questions yesterday. Discernment is countercultural because it takes time.

The discernment process enables groups to delve deeper into their lives, to find the complexity and richness inside themselves, and to be led by God into new discoveries. A church cannot expect to receive instant answers to its questions. The questions that emerge about the challenges lead to complexity, not to simple yes-or-no answers. So then, what questions should be framed?

Corporate spiritual discernment flows out of four primary questions:

God, what is your yearning for our church?

God, what would you have us do?

God, how would you have us grow spiritually?

God, how would you have us change?

These questions are the "bottom line" questions. In the midst of the church's issues and challenges these primary questions are always at the center because they do not limit God to any particular issue or challenge. God's vision is bigger than human vision could ever be. Hear God's words in Isaiah 55:8:

> For my thoughts are not your thoughts,
> nor are your ways my ways, says the Lord.

Specific questions, such as, *God, should we hire a youth director?* or *God, should we have contemporary or blended worship?* place limits on God. The area has already been chosen, and the emphasis is already placed on human ways. The four primary questions above open the team to God's ways and new possibilities, wholeness, and life. Everything a congregation faces fits into these questions, especially the first one: *God, what is your yearning for our church/organization?*

The categories listed in the "Naming and Describing the Issues" exercise on page 49 name the main challenges a church faces. Work in the discernment process is not seeking to fix a specific issue (such as starting a contemporary worship service or not) but to listen to God's leadership in addressing the issue (*God, what is your yearning for our worship?*). Keep the challenges that have been identified in mind as prayers are offered about the primary question of God's yearning for the church.

Expect God to lead in new directions utilizing your strengths and transforming the challenges. The challenges need to be held lightly. God will often communicate, *I am not calling you to address that specific challenge. I am asking you to minister out of your gifts and passions. The challenge you have listed does not match your gifts.*

Here is an example of such a transformation in a church community with whom we worked:

This church named attracting more youth as their dream and as a challenge. They wanted more young people and their families, but they struggled because the megachurch in town already drew most of the youth to their strong Bible studies and activities.

As we all worked through the discernment process, the discernment team members came to realize that serving older adults was where their gifts and also their passion lay. After much prayer, they came to understand that God was not calling them to "grow" a large youth group. Instead, God was asking them to serve older adults and to allow space and ministry opportunities for the older adults to mentor youth in the community. The mentoring was done as a way to connect older adults and youth in the community without any expectation that the youth would start attending their church services. The discernment team realized they couldn't compete with the megachurch's youth group. More importantly, God was not asking them to enter into competition. Their process of discernment moved along more smoothly as soon as they shifted the emphasis on "youth" to a larger perspective that identified ways to connect and mentor the youth in the community through the gifts of ministry from older adults.

Naming the church's challenges is essential, and the strengths and challenges of your church need to be lifted up under the rubric of the primary questions about God's yearning. Making a Discernment Prayer Card for everyone in the discernment group can be helpful. Each person can place the card where it will serve as a daily discernment prayer reminder. The team members can use the cards as a tool for daily prayer and meditation on the questions.

Discernment Prayer Card
List the grouped challenges your church is facing based on the "Naming and Describing the Issues" exercise.

Commit to this prayer:
I will read scripture, meditate, and pray daily, listening for God's guidance on the following primary questions:

> *God, what is your yearning for our church?*
> *God, what would you have us do?*
> *God, how would you have us grow spiritually?*
> *God, how would you have us change?*

Dreaming

Once the current situation has been named, the team can take some time to dream a little. God uses creative abilities as an avenue for groups to uncover God's vision for the future. The Holy Spirit works through imagination, and dreaming opens the team's creativity for the Spirit to move. At the same time, naming personal dreams and visions brings them to the surface. As group members name personal dreams and visions and offer them up to God, these dreams are less likely to become hidden personal agendas. Discernment doesn't preclude dreaming. The key is turning the visions over to God and then listening for God's dream in the midst. The following exercise encourages naming the team's dreams for the church.

Dreaming

What dream(s) does the team have for the church?
First answer this question as individuals, then respond to it as a whole group.

Where do you sense the Holy Spirit in the midst of the group's dreaming?

Prayer
God, we offer our dreams to you. Help us to see them as human visions and to open them up to your power, creativity, and transformation. Guide us now to see your dream for us. Amen.

Here is a report from another church we worked with:

> A few years ago our church began a visioning process. We divided the church into cottage communities. These groups met several times to ask a question: *If the Holy Spirit were allowed to move in our midst, what would our church look like?* Each group then entered into discussion and prayer. As each cottage group reported back, we were amazed at the similarity of ideas and themes that came forth.

This congregation took the time to stop, pray, and dream in the presence of the Holy Spirit. The people took time to listen to the movement of the Holy Spirit, and they began to recognize the Spirit working through their imagination and creativity. They saw glimpses of visions they had never thought possible. They felt the power of God when they allowed the Holy Spirit to move in their midst.

Naming the current situation and then dreaming dreams are both part of naming the issues. Now it is time to put this issue into a context that will uncover God's yearning for the church's unfolding future.

CHAPTER FIVE

Centering

Introduction

WITH THE MAIN ISSUES for discernment named and framed, it is time to become aware of the values and assumptions that affect the process of discernment. When you set out in a canoe, you must find your center or balancing point as you move through the water. If you lean one way too far, the canoe tips over. Especially if the waters are rough and the rapids swift, you need to adjust position continually in order to find the proper balance. Discernment is similar to balancing in a canoe. As your discernment team moves through the waters of exploration, you become more aware of centering on God and finding your balancing point. When the balance shifts one way or another based on feelings or values within the team rather than God's centering point, the canoe/team will tip over.

Remember, discernment involves hearing what God wants. Questions about where the discernment group finds its balancing point need to be asked. For example: *Is our church centered where Christ would lead us? Are we seeking guidance from something or someone other than God? Are we avoiding some things we need to address?*

Few people realize that when they sign onto a discernment team, they will be asked to change and grow into a deeper relationship with Christ. You were probably not warned that serving in this responsible capacity can be a life-altering experience! The movement of centering calls for giving up preconceived notions about leadership skills and potential outcomes. The process in this circle takes you into a listening, learning posture that allows the Holy Spirit to lead the group.

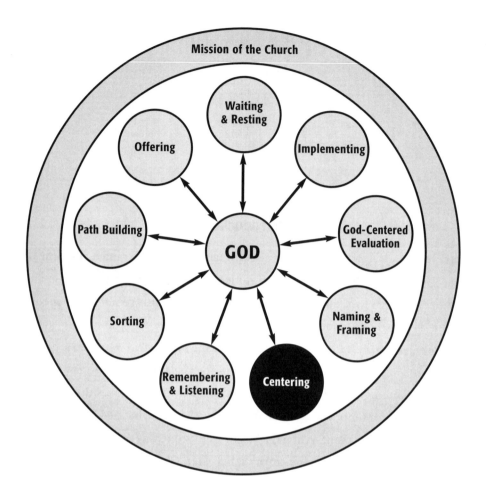

Centering requires letting go of "my" agendas and shedding anything that stands in the way of focusing on God's will as the ultimate value. The process of centering is not easy, nor does it come quickly. Yet this refocusing activity is essential for discernment. A familiar scripture passage informs centering:

> You shall love the Lord your God with all your heart, and with all your soul, and with all your strength, and with all your mind, and your neighbor as yourself. (Luke 10:27)

The first part of this text reminds us that we are to focus on God who is in the center of everything! Humans are called to love God with all that they have and are. When we love God in this way, God becomes the center. People are drawn to what God desires for them and want what God wants. Only when God becomes that "balancing point" for the discernment team can the members begin to know God's longing for the mission of their church.

The second part of this text, about loving your neighbor, is also essential. In the discernment process, the neighbor is no farther away than the person sitting in the next chair. Individuals, when they become part of the leadership group entering into discernment, are called upon to grow and connect with the other members of the team. When you begin your work, you know the people in the group at one level, but discernment calls for a deeper level of sharing and listening. As members of the group go deeper, everyone gains companions for the journey. Loving your neighbor as yourself also means learning to trust others.

> A church had been doing worshipful-work and discernment for several years when we were invited to work with them. We asked people in the church what was the key to their ability to enter this new way of life together. They replied, "Discernment worked when we finally learned to trust each other and the work of each committee. We began to trust that each committee had been praying and listening to God. We were then free to listen to God at the governing board level when we didn't have to scrutinize the work of each committee."

These people had learned to trust and love one another in the mission they accomplished together. Their center shifted. They no longer worried about whether the other members were doing their jobs correctly. They realized God was in the center for everyone.

Holy Indifference

One of the ways to begin to discover the source of guidance for the group is to focus on what has been called "holy indifference." Holy indifference requires letting go of personal agendas and becoming indifferent to any choice except what God wants. It sounds easy, but it's not!

This principle of spiritual discernment was named by Ignatius of Loyola in the 1600s in his classic text *Spiritual Exercises*. Holy indifference is a positive stance in the process of centering. "Ignatian indifference is a state of inner free-dom, openness, and balance" that encourages the discerner not to incline more toward one opinion than to another. "Indifference is a poised freedom that pre-serves our ability to go one way or another depending on the indication of God's lead. By calling for indifference, Ignatius is calling for a willingness right from the start to be influenced in the process by God's guidance."[1]

Holy indifference as a way of being can also be called "shedding" and is defined as "naming and laying aside anything that will deter the person or group from focusing on God's will as the ultimate value."[2] By letting go of agen-das, shedding enables an individual or group to desire only what God desires.

Indifference carries a negative meaning in today's society. For most people, it means not caring about something one way or another. However, holy indif-ference means not caring about the outcome, *except* as God wants the outcome. The point is not to direct the results, *except* as God directs. Holy indifference means becoming indifferent to any outcome *except* God's longing for the church. Coming to the point of holy indifference centers the team's focus on God. But grasping the concept and living into holy indifference is challenging. The fol-lowing statements illustrate the kind of roadblocks a team might encounter as members attempt this shift:

- We will do anything God wants *except close the doors of our church*.
- We will look at all the possibilities; *however, we need to put more weight on church growth*.
- We will do anything God wants, but *we really need a young pastor*.
- I am excited about developing ministry programs for the community. *I am concerned* that some of the groups will spill coffee on the carpet or allow their children to tear things up.

The words and phrases italicized above signal that individuals or the group have not reached holy indifference. People are still placing their own will in the center.

In developing holy indifference, the team needs to adopt the basic assump-tion that anything other than God's yearning is not where the team wants to go in visioning for the church. When the team enters into discernment, all members need to be willing to say, "No matter the outcome of the process, it will be okay" instead of saying, for instance, "We will do anything God wants this church to do . . . except close our doors."

One way to discover where the stumbling blocks to holy indifference exist requires writing down the content of these issues; then the team will be able to explore them. As the group discusses issues within the church, differing points of view will emerge. Reflecting on such discussions, particularly if they are intense or they continue in the parking lot after meetings, will identify the difficult areas. Realizing that each person brings agendas and assumptions to the discussions is part of beginning to see where each person is called to let go. In a corporate setting, this requires talking with each other on a deep level, sharing fears and desires. For example, one discernment team member in a church shared this story:

> My parents were part of the core group who started this church, and I am fearful I will be in the group that God calls to close the church. When I discuss these feelings with others on the team, I find out that I am not alone. When I bring this fear and put it "on the table," it is less likely to get in the way of hearing God, because others know how I feel or may be feeling the same way. When I find there are similar feelings in the group, we can work together to let those feelings go.

When individuals address desires openly, team members can begin to listen to what the other person is saying rather than worry about the other's hidden agendas.

Holy indifference challenges the discerning team to let go, one by one, of each of those places where its will stands in the center. If the team will follow this process, eventually they understand that no matter where God calls, God has taken into consideration objections and deeply felt desires. No matter where God is leading, God gives strength for the journey. The following exercise starts the team in this direction. Members will name places where individuals and the team itself need to work on letting go in order to reach holy indifference.

". . . not my will but yours be done."

—Luke 22:42

Holy Indifference

- Lift up one of the named issues that is a focus for discernment.
- List on newsprint all of the possible solutions (good and bad) you can see at this time.
- Prioritize the list.
- Ask the group to discuss the probable results if the bottom item happened or the top priority didn't happen.

- Next discuss what holy indifference means and allow for silent reflection.
- Have *individuals* write answers to the following two questions:

    What am *I* having a hard time letting go?

    What exceptions are preventing *me* from reaching holy indifference?

- Reconvene the whole group for discussion of people's answers.
- Then ask the *group* the same questions, followed by a time for silent reflection.

    What are *we* having a hard time letting go?

    What exceptions are preventing *us* from reaching holy indifference?

- Write a prayer to ask for God's help and grace in reaching a place of holy indifference.

The discernment team probably will need to repeat this prayer on a regular basis because holy indifference is difficult to achieve.

God calls each person to let go of objections, to let go of fears, and to trust deeply that God's yearning and Christ's call to us will be enough. The discerning team will be surrounded and supported by the Holy Spirit in such ways that it can move through fears to trust in God's sufficiency. God calls each person and the group to face the fears and to examine what holds them back from walking boldly into God's future. God asks for trust at a level that is new territory for many people, but the Spirit encourages them to enter into a relationship with God that they may not have thought possible. Fears, objections, and desires are to be placed on the "offering table" for God to transform.

In addition to the group's personal desires and fears, people typically have assumptions about how God will respond to the issues that have been named and framed. It is normal to expect God to answer prayers in our human framework and timetable. Sometimes the expected answers don't arrive, sometimes no answer is forthcoming, and sometimes the answers are not what was hoped. Rather than conclude that the experiment in corporate discernment has failed, that God has betrayed the team, or that some members have not been listening to God, perhaps the team can try to see where God *is* working. God may be issuing an invitation to go deeper into prayer and to let go of preset timetables and agendas. Perhaps God is responding with an answer for which no one is yet prepared.[3]

The group can return to the fundamental assumption that when they ask God to be part of the discernment process, God will be. Members need to remind themselves to be open to God's leading rather than remain bound by expectations about how God "should" act. Growth in discipleship calls for being open to the Spirit's leading. Jesus was continually pushing the Pharisees to look outside the boxes they built around their faith. Discernment calls for looking outside the boxes of human imagination into places only God can imagine. Holding back with a "yes, but . . ." restricts the future to the framework of human design.

We build boxes not only with fears and desires but also with values. Often the three are connected. Reaching holy indifference is difficult when people hold one value or one thing above another. For example, when churches measure success in numbers rather than depth of relationship, it is difficult to let go of the growth desires. It is not unusual for the biggest stumbling blocks in the discernment process to be centered on core values.

Core Values

Core values are the ones that have been developed over the years and have become the pillars of faith and life. When a person says, "Of course, we will need to _____," the blank probably comes out of a core value. For example, suppose a budget deficit is an issue. When someone comments, "Of course, if the evangelism committee would bring in twenty new families, we wouldn't have a problem," he or she is expressing the core value that success is measured in numbers.

Values are important to people as guiding principles in their lives; they function as instructions on how to live. However, the core values held so dearly may not express God's vision for a church. Team members may need to loosen their hold on the bedrock of their values in order to hear God's voice calling them into new arenas. For example, a core value may be that a successful church is a large church, and that in order to be successful, this church needs to grow. And yet, God may be calling this church to a ministry of growing disciples to maturity, and outreach to the community. In this case, numbers do not measure success. "Success" may be more closely related to how well the church helps local families receive adequate health care for their children.

The core values of the individuals and of the team need to be identified while God's yearning for the mission of the church is uncovered. Each individual brings core values to the process. For example, one person may declare that the church *must* participate in a particular overseas mission project. The corporate body also brings values to the process, such as a conviction that their minister must have a PhD in preaching.

Review the exercise in which you characterized the church as a person. Items listed there may very well reveal core values the church holds. For example, if the group understands the church to be like a highly competent person, then the quality of competence in facing challenges is a core value. Or if this church/person is highly energetic, activities may be valued over contemplation.

Take time to work through the following exercise to see what values rise to the surface for the discernment team.

Core Values

Prayer
God, help us begin to recognize our individual and corporate core values so that they will not to get in the way of hearing your word for us. Amen.

Allow silence for reflection on core values.

Ask *individuals* to respond to the following question:
> What core values are important to me as we seek God's desire for our church?

Share individual core values around the table.

Ask *the group* to respond to the following question:
>What core values are important to this congregation as we seek God's desire for our church?

Then ask the group to identify which core values rise to the surface as most influential in this congregation.

Remember that holding core values lightly initially may feel uncomfortable. Once everyone in the group realizes that the values are personal or corporate ("mine" or "ours") rather than divine (God's), it may be easier to let go of them if God calls the group to do so. For example, suppose a core value for a church is leadership by a highly educated pastor, usually holding a PhD. Now the church operates in an urban community with critical needs. God is calling the church to stay in its location, and the only available pastor with urban ministry experience does not have as much education as members of the congregation. Is the church's core value about a pastor's education level held above God's call?

As a team works to identify and live a life of discernment, the members will find their priorities changing and their core values becoming less important than they once were.

Values Clarification

The techniques of values clarification offer a form for group process in discussions about individual and corporate values. *Values Clarification: A Practical, Action-Directed Workbook* (Simon, Howe, Kirschenbaum) provides useful techniques the team can adopt to design their own values clarification exercises.

Values clarification techniques allow members of the group to recognize the places where they are similar and where they are different. As people begin to trust one another, the activities can be used to encourage deeper conversation about these values. The purpose of the clarification activities is to name the core values of the group, and then of the church. Once the group identifies core values, members are better prepared to make choices about strengthening or shifting values as God leads.

As the team clarifies their values, members will come to the place where holy indifference and centering on God become critical. The whole discernment process must be given to God. The team, like Jesus, must say, "not my will but yours be done" (Luke 22:42). Core values are named so that they can be instructive, but they also need to be available to God to change. In order to hear God's longing for the life of the church, the team needs to hold values lightly and work through the process of holy indifference.

CHAPTER SIX

Remembering and Listening

Introduction

INFORMATION GATHERED in this circle of the discernment process will further define the church's identity. The team will recognize the history of the church and community and listen for the underlying messages. Attention moves to voices from the past and voices from the team. Discernment cannot be done in a vacuum. First it is critical to listen to the church's history, to understand its past. Then listening to people in the church and in the community will clarify who the church is today. Taking the time to explore the past can reveal what gifts the church has to offer. Listening to church members refines the sense of where the gifts lie now. Talking with the larger community puts all the gifts into the context of the world around the church.

Discernment is about "starting with God's gifts, not our actions."[1] Claiming what God has already given a faith community helps in naming the church's identity. God's call for each church is based on the gifts each congregation has to offer, and each church is unique. Every church is called to be faithful to who and what God has created it to be.

Separating the past from the present can be tricky, especially in the church. When the team listens to members of the congregation talk about joys and struggles in the church, the information is often based on past events. Therefore, *remembering* and *listening* have been combined into the same circle. The activities in this chapter are set up as independent exercises. However, based on the church and the way the team is approaching the discernment process, more than one activity may be done in any given setting.

> **Note:** The movement of listening and remembering is crucial because most of the data is collected in this part of the process. Therefore, this chapter includes many exercises. The chapter may appear overwhelming, but these exercises need not all be accomplished in a short time period. Space them out and plan for rest and reflection between exercises. Choose someone on the team to document the information collected in the exercises and distribute it to members of the discernment team in a timely manner.

Biblical Call to Remember

The church encounters the call to remember God's mighty acts throughout the Bible. The theme of remembering permeates the book of Deuteronomy, especially in chapters 8 and 9 when God calls the Israelites to remember all that God has done for them. The people are challenged to remember and not forget that God acted in their lives to bring them out of slavery in Egypt and into the Promised Land.

We're easily distracted in the life of the church and can forget to whom the church belongs, who has acted mightily in the life of the community and its members. Exodus and Joshua specifically instruct the faith community to remember and retell the story. Passover becomes an act of remembrance as the people are encouraged to "re-member" the story and tell of God's faithfulness when the children ask what they are celebrating (Exod. 12:26-27). The memorial made out of twelve stones from the Jordan River provides another opportunity to remember. When the children ask what the stones are for, the people tell the story about God cutting off the waters of the Jordan River so that the people could pass through on dry land (Josh. 4:4-7).

The Psalms also emphasize remembering and repeat the charge not to forget. Many psalms recall God's faithfulness to the community of faith or the individual. Some call on God not to forget the relationship with God's people (Ps. 9:9-12, 18). Others feature the theme of remembering Israel's historical relationship with God (Pss. 106, 136). The psalms were intended to be repeated over and over to remind us of God's leading in the past, of God's faithfulness, and of

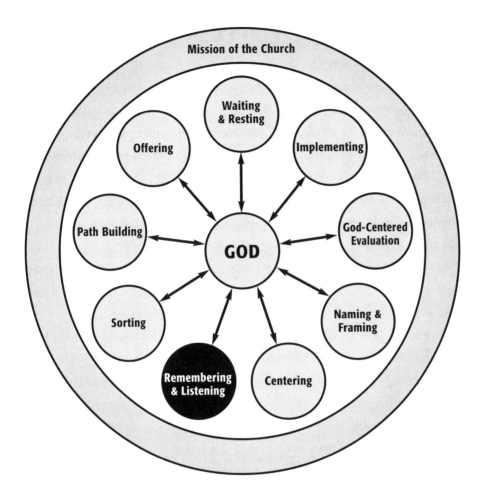

God's love and grace (Ps. 107). They remind the church that it is not alone and that God will act in its future as the church discerns God's longing for it. Christmas, Easter, and Pentecost offer Christians similar acts of remembrance during the year. These holy days celebrate anew the major events in our shared history: with each one the church retells the story of God's interaction with humankind.

The Lord's Table becomes a dynamic remembering for Christians. In Luke 22:19 Jesus says, "This is my body, which is given for you. Do this in remembrance of me." Therefore, every time the faith community comes together around the Communion table they "re-member" that night when Jesus had supper with the community of men and women around him. The story is repeated, and all the meaning wrapped up in that simple, yet complex, event is remembered.

The Holy Spirit

The Holy Spirit is active in the process of discernment. The Spirit comes to humans in many forms, so the team needs to be prepared to listen to words from unexpected places and unexpected people. As the process unfolds, sometimes individuals on the team will report being caught off guard by the words of a song or portions of a worship service that seem to be speaking directly to them.

The discernment team can use art to assist in the discernment process. Ellen Morseth in *Ritual & the Arts in Spiritual Discernment* suggests finding a picture of a path, road, gate, or other quiet meditative scene. While gazing at the picture, team members can contemplate questions such as, *Where do you find yourself in the picture and why? Where do you think the church is on the path and why?* Often, honest responses to a piece of art point to individuals' feelings about an issue or to their fears. Val Isenhower is a landscape photographer with several pictures appropriate for the discernment process on her Web site www.visenhowerphotography.com.

The Holy Spirit prompts the team through continued reading of the biblical stories.

The Holy Spirit prompts interior feelings through art, music, and pictures. Each person on the team can learn to pay attention to his or her feelings and to talk about them. The Holy Spirit will often give individuals a sense of ease or un-ease about a decision, so listening to feelings becomes worthwhile.

Music and dreams also may be vehicles for the Holy Spirit's communication. Paying attention to the words or themes the team repeatedly notices in music—whether during their meetings or in other places—aids in discussion of feelings. The members of the team might try writing down their dreams to see if they are pertinent to the discernment process.

When the discernment team members honestly share their interior feelings and what they are hearing, they often will discover they are not alone. When one person feels uncomfortable about something, often others do too. When one person feels drawn toward a particular action or decision, often others are too.

Finally, the Holy Spirit prompts the team through continued reading of the biblical stories. When the team uses the spiritual practice of *lectio divina* to slow down the reading, and ponders words in the biblical passage, the Holy Spirit can be part of the conversation. The Spirit will emphasize words from the biblical reading that are often echoed in team members' lives if the team has the ears and the patience to hear.

Remembering Our Story

Storytelling always has been significant in human history. Grandparents, parents, and storytellers in communities pass down narratives from generation to generation. Storytelling reminds individuals who they are. For the community of faith, stories remind us to whom we belong. Stories transmit history to each successive generation, both for teaching purposes and for entertainment. The act of telling the narratives over and over becomes a way to "re-member" an event, to put all the pieces back together so that we bring the event into our present. Remembering helps churches look at their past to see where they have been and to know who they are now.

> We worked with a church that was only twenty-five years old. Even though most of the founding members were still part of the church, the congregation had not thought about their beginnings for a long time. We led them through a storytelling exercise to recover their past. In telling the story they remembered that they were formed as a small church focused on a family atmosphere. Children were treated as though they were members of every family. When teenagers went off to college, they received mail from many members of the church. Everyone knew one another. Community was important. The sense of God's presence had been very strong in the early years. As church members remembered their past, they realized that their identity revolved around being a small family-oriented church. Suddenly their dream of becoming a much larger church and reaching out to singles didn't seem as important. They discovered if their dreams were realized, they would lose their gift of offering a small-community atmosphere for families who were looking for that type of setting. They valued the times they felt God's touch in their families' lives.

Maureen Conroy reminds us that "God's touch, though taking place in a moment of time, lives on within us forever."[2] When a church remembers the times members have experienced God, they reenact those events in their hearts and minds. The stories remind them of God's grace and love and the fact that they are not alone. The remembering brings to a conscious level that which has touched the life of the church in the past. Church members remember that they are children of God and that they are beloved (see chapter 3). God has touched the church and led people in the past and will be faithful to do so in the present and future.

Telling the Story

Many churches have written histories of their congregation, which provide valuable information for the discernment team. Often a history includes the church's original mission statement. Most churches take care to update and write current mission statements but give them little attention afterward. Since the discernment team is listening for God's guidance, paying attention to the content of any available mission statements can be pertinent.

However, the team needs to hear the story in the words of current members also. These persons need to be placed in the context of the church's history. Where has God been at work in recent times as well as in the past? The time line exercise, based on an idea by Chuck Olsen, is a way for the discernment team to tell the story in their own words and to see recurring themes.[3]

Time Line Exercise

Preparation

Have current and past mission statements available. Tape several pieces of newsprint together, or use a roll of butcher paper. Put several tables end to end and lay the paper out on top. On the left side of the paper place a vertical slash mark and the date the church was founded. On the right side place a vertical slash mark with the current date. Draw a horizontal line between the two slash marks. Place vertical slash marks at decade intervals between the founding date and today. Label each decade.

Exercise

Ask each individual to enter on the time line the date he or she was baptized in this particular church or joined the church (approximate date and name). Next, let each person add significant moments for them as individuals in the church. As a group, remember and add significant points in the life of the church. Include pastoral leadership, new mission statements, times of struggle, and times when God's presence was felt in the life of the church.

Look at the information on the time line and discuss the following questions:
- When were the major turning points in the life of the church?

- When did the church sense God's presence?

- When did the church perceive God as absent?

- How did the mission statements reflect current circumstances in the congregation?

- What themes emerge?

- What do you find surprising on the time line?

- What is missing on the time line? Add other elements you want included.

Chuck Olsen offers another style of storytelling called "and then . . . but before that."[4] This method provides a way to fill in gaps in the church's story, because it acknowledges that everyone holds a piece of the history. It is helpful to use

- when a past story within the church's history is troubling and more information is needed;
- when any story within the history of the church needs to be told in detail;
- any time the church wants to hear the richness of its history, especially those times when God's presence was felt;
- when teaching new members and children about the church.

The time line brings stories to the surface that may need to be explored further. The next step, then, is to tell these stories as a group. The following exercise amplifies the information gathered in the time-line exercise; it is best done during a subsequent meeting.

"And then . . . but before that"

One person begins the story of the church, starting at any point in time, by saying one or two lines. Going in order around the room, the next person says either

- *"and then"* and continues with the story adding one or two sentences about subsequent events; or
- *"but before that "* and recounts incidents prior to the first told in one or two sentences

People may also preface their contribution with other phrases such as *"and at the same time."* Continue the storytelling until all pertinent information has been shared.

Discussion
- What have we learned from this storytelling?

- What new information came to the surface?

- How was God active in this event?

- How does this information change the team's outlook on the church's history?

By shedding light on the past, this method of storytelling often uncovers missing information needed in the discernment process. We heard an account of this exercise from a church that had experienced a major conflict in the past. The leadership decided it would be helpful to use "and then . . . but before that" as a tool for healing and moving on. After the church retold the story, a person in the group said, "Now I understand how I was a part of the conflict. I am sorry for my actions, and I will work toward being more open to our future."

Telling the story in this way can sometimes clarify why members in the past blocked certain actions. One church learned from recounting a conflict over recarpeting the church parlor.

The trustees asked the members to vote on three choices of carpet. Each of the carpet styles matched the architectural style and use of the room. The trustees thought they were being open by asking for a vote on the final carpet choice rather than making the decision themselves. They were surprised when a conflict developed. Nevertheless, the vote was taken one Sunday after worship. A "winner" was declared, and the parlor was recarpeted. It wasn't until later when the story was told that the problem was clarified. The individuals who had selected the original carpet for the parlor were still church members. They didn't care which carpet was chosen, but they thought they should have been consulted and their prior research shared.

The conflict might have been avoided if the trustees had stopped the decision-making process as soon as conflict arose and asked some questions.

God's Faithfulness

The team has already talked about times when God's faithfulness and God's saving grace have been experienced. Remembering these times and referring to them will bolster the group throughout the process.

God's Faithfulness
- When was God's presence felt in the life of the church?
- Tell the stories of what was going on and how God's presence was experienced.
- Add to these stories as the team walks through the discernment process.
- Recall these stories when the team feels bogged down in the process.

Biblical Reflection

By using the biblical stories the discernment team can begin to sense some leading toward possible paths ahead. The voices in the Bible supply foundational understandings of the church's history and current identity.

The Bible is living testimony to God's faithfulness as well as to the actions of the community of faith and its interactions with the triune God. The Bible lives today because so often people find themselves in the text; it is full of what are called *paradigm stories*. In such stories the issues of our biblical ancestors are echoed in the issues of contemporary people. Reading and hearing paradigm stories, as well as studying those who have gone before us, illuminate the challenges that a church faces today.

Biblical Reflection

The Past

- Think of a significant event in the history of the local church. What biblical story does it bring to mind?
- Tell the two stories.
- In what ways does the biblical story intersect with the history of the church?
- What character(s) in the biblical story does the church most resemble?
- What does the biblical story say about how God acted in the life of the church? What else can be learned from the story?

The Present

- Think about the present state of the faith community. What biblical story comes to mind?
- Follow the process above.

Application

- How do the stories shed light on the challenges the church is facing and on the questions that have been framed for spiritual discernment?

Listening to the Congregation

Up to this point, the team has focused on laying a foundation for discernment, listening to one another, recalling the church's history, and paying attention to the movement of the Holy Spirit. Now the team will listen to the congregation.

In order for members of the congregation to be comfortable sharing, it is essential that they feel heard. Spend time reviewing attentive listening skills:

- Face the person who is talking.
- Look the person in the eye.
- Show the person that he or she is being heard by nodding your head or giving verbal cues, such as "okay."

- Listen fully without thinking about your response.
- Be aware of the tone of voice.
- Notice what the person is not saying.
- Observe body language.
- Ask the Spirit to help you "hear" what the person wants to communicate.

Adapt these skills to the cultural patterns of the church. Remind team members to listen to the members of the congregation with the same attentiveness they used when listening to one another's faith journeys earlier (see chapter 2).

The team will now begin conducting listening sessions in order to gather observations, history, feelings, and insights from the congregation. The following listening session example presents one method for hearing the stories of the past while offering an opportunity to hear the pains, sorrows, joys, traditions, and symbols within the events described. The session also serves as a means to hear the dreams and visions of the congregation. Each listening session focuses on four questions:

- What of the past has shaped this congregation?
- What has this congregation struggled with in the past?
- Where has God been active in this congregation?
- If the Holy Spirit were allowed to move, what do you think this congregation would look like?

One method of organizing listening sessions is to divide the congregation into small groups with no more than twenty in each group. Assign two team members to each group. These persons will facilitate a listening session with their group. Two team members are assigned to each group so that one can be attentive in listening and the other person can act as the recorder. The sessions can be organized in different ways. Here are two:

- Divide into the small groups after a church dinner.
- Team members invite their assigned group for a meal or for coffee and discussion in a home setting.

Before organizing the sessions, inform the congregation about the listening sessions and the purpose for them. Make sure everyone in the church, both members and friends, is invited to participate. Don't forget the youth and the children. Record who is present at each listening session. Contact those who did not attend and ask them the questions in person. If they choose not to respond, let it go and ask God to be with them.

Each listening session lasts about an hour and a half. Following each session, the team members write a summary report that highlights the content of the meeting. The reports are collated and distributed to the whole discernment team for discussion at the next team meeting.

Remember, these are *listening* sessions. Now is not the time to respond to individual comments. People will shut down and stop responding to the questions honestly if they feel they are being judged.

Listening Session*

Begin the session with prayer:
Loving God, we are seeking your vision for our church. Give us courage to answer the questions honestly. Help us to hear one another with love and compassion. Give us wisdom to know when to be silent. Help us to see your work in our midst. In the name of the One who taught us to hear, Jesus Christ. Amen.

Share these instructions with the gathered group:
As you know, we have made a commitment to move in the direction God would have this church go, rather than where we as humans want to go. With the Holy Spirit as our guide, we have embarked on a process of discernment to see where God is leading us. We feel it is important to hear everyone's voice. So we are conducting listening sessions in small groups to include the whole church. We are gathered tonight to hear your responses to some questions. We will share the responses with the discernment team. However, please know, we will not attach names to the comments when we take them back to the team.

We will do our best to hear what you are saying. We ask that everyone listen to whoever is speaking. Give each person your respect and attention. The answers are based on what you see, feel, and observe. Therefore there are no right or wrong answers to the questions. This is not a time for debate or discussion; it is a time for listening.

1. What from the past has shaped this congregation?
   a. *People*—those no longer in the church, through death or leaving; those whom you knew or know about; those whose invisible hand continues to help shape this church; names, and a brief description of memorable attributes.
   b. *Traditions*—those happenings that are part of the "wells of vitality" of this congregation; those practices that are "just the way we do it around here."
   c. *Symbols*—material objects that help define this congregation; the items include but are not limited to symbols of traditional religious nature.

2. What has this congregation struggled with in the past?
   a. Has there been a degree of resolution?
   b. What are the residual effects?
   c. What have been the learnings?
   d. What needs to be resolved before moving into the future?

3. What has the congregation celebrated in the past?
   a. Significant anniversaries (e.g., 25, 50, 100)
   b. Retiring the mortgage
   c. Specific events, such as, pastor-led changes, mergers

4. Where has God been active in this congregation?
   a. What biblical stories come to mind in past events?
   b. Has God felt absent at any point?
   c. How do you know God is present?

5. If the Holy Spirit were allowed to move, what do you think this church would look like?

Thank everyone for coming. *Conclude with prayer*:
God, go with us as we continue this process of discernment. We ask for healing of the wounds we have heard about today. We give you thanks for how you have acted in our history. We ask for continued guidance as we move into our future. In Christ's name we pray, Amen.

* Questions 1 and 2 are adapted from materials by Angus W. McGregor, Interim Ministry Training, August, 2003.

A lot of time has been spent listening to the internal voices in the church. Moving beyond the congregation out into the community is the next critical undertaking.

Listening to the Community

The team steps outside the walls of the church to gain a different perspective. Congregational members do not hold all the knowledge required to uncover God's mission for the church. The team needs to hear what the community says about its needs and about the church.

What voices in the community need to be heard? Take some time for the team to make a list of people to contact and then make specific assignments within the team. The following is a suggested starter list. The final list depends on your particular church and community. Add to this list as appropriate.

- Mayor
- Police chief or sheriff
- City council members
- School superintendent and local principal(s)
- Service agency leaders
- Homeless shelter
- Food bank
- United Way, Catholic Charities, etc.
- Other church leaders
- Clergy group
- Interfaith agency
- Pastors of prominent churches in town

Recommended interview instructions:

- Call the community leader.
- Tell the person who you are and where you are from.
- Explain that your church is in a discernment process to see where God is leading. You are seeking information from the community leaders.

- Ask if she or he would be willing to help.

- Set up an appointment.

- Respect the person by showing up on time and keeping the appointment as brief as possible.

- Write a thank-you note after your visit.

Use the following two fundamental questions as a guideline for discussion with community leaders.[5] Add questions appropriate to your own community and your church or organization. Print out several copies of the final list of questions for team members to use as a reference. Each team member records interview responses on the page for reporting back to the team. Once the interviews are completed, the team will meet to discuss them and to get a sense of the responses and the needs in their community.

Community Calls

Person to Interview: _____

Interview Questions:

1. What do you see as the most important needs in _____?
   (Your City/Town)

2. How do you think _____ could help meet those needs?
   (Your Church's Name)

Gather all the input you have heard from the various voices. Listen to the responses and pray over them, but do not begin sorting the information yet. That process will come later. Ask God to help you see what and who is missing. Do you need to talk to the neighbors around your church? Do you need to include voices of the unchurched?

All the material collected through these activities forms the database of voices for the discernment team. Some voices may trigger emotions among the team members. Sometimes the feelings will be remembered grief from the church's past. Sometimes the feelings will be excitement as the needs and ideas come together for future possibilities. Sometimes the feelings may be overwhelming when many voices are heard. The team members need to allow time for the multiplicity of the voices to settle and for the data to be sorted. The process does take time. Surrounding the process with prayer keeps all of the voices in perspective.

Healing the Past and Celebrating

As we have worked in churches, often stories of pain come to the surface. Wounds from the past that members thought were healed open up again. Sometimes struggles that people considered settled flare up, and the church finds the fire was never extinguished completely. At other times grief over a loss in the church may be stirred, and the pain is felt again. Some churches find that significant events were never celebrated appropriately. Don't be surprised if such matters arise. These discoveries are part of understanding the church's identity and ultimately uncovering God's longing for the church.

When feelings of pain, anger, grief, or loss from the past rise to the surface, incorporate them into group discussion. Don't ignore the feelings, but lay them out and then take them to God. Bring the healing power of God into the midst. The Christian tradition of worship can be beneficial at this time. Design services as needed for:

- grief over lost members or former pastors (appendix D)
- reconciliation services where forgiveness is needed
- healing services for wounds that haven't healed
- celebration of significant events that have been forgotten

Often the act of acknowledging pains and sorrows in worship provides the healing people need. When these times of upheaval are ignored, they tend to grow and take on a life of their own. Remember, God is loving and full of grace and wants to help churches become whole.

Prayer for Remembering and Listening

Loving God, full of compassion and grace, walk beside us as we remember our past and listen to the voices around us. We know there have been pains and sorrows in our history and that as we listen to these stories there may still be strong feelings around them. Give us strength to hear what we need to hear. Give us wisdom to listen with compassion. Help us heal wounds and celebrate gifts. In the name of the One who offered compassion throughout his ministry, Jesus Christ. Amen.

Learning to Trust

So far the team has been listening to the past and gathering information. Even though team members may not agree with everything they have heard, they have listened and recorded the voices. The context has been the past and the present, not the future. Before moving into the next part of the process, the team needs to address any fears that have arisen and to trust God with them.

People often reveal their fears with a "yes, but" response. The "but" suggests why something cannot be accomplished. Or someone may say, "I don't want our church to do that, because. . . ." The phrase "but what if" may also signal fear. Individuals' fears arise based on experiences in this particular church as well as in other churches where team members have belonged. The past experiences and fears limit the ability of the team to address the corporate discernment process. Attempts to play it safe, to avoid venturing into dangerous territory, can handicap the team.

Fears also arise when the team senses loss of control. Suddenly the team realizes that if it moves on, it is no longer in charge. God may be calling the church into areas where the team does not feel competent. Fear might be prompted by the changes foreseen and the difficulty the congregation will experience in making such changes.

God's yearning calls upon the team to learn how to set aside fears and to trust in God alone. Although setting aside fears is not an easy task, the call to trust is clear. Remember that in the Bible when the angels appear, they say, "Do not be afraid" (Matt. 1:20; 28:5; and Luke 1:13, 30). In the biblical stories, as well as those of the congregation, God's voice calls to humans to live on the other side of their fears and to live into God's vision for the future. The following liturgy may be used often, whenever fears arise in the process.

Fears

Ask each person on the team to list fears related to the discernment process and God's yearning for the church.

Share these fears with one another if people are willing to do so, but do not discuss them. Remember, what is frightening to one person may not be for another. Listen attentively and hold the fears up to God in prayer. Share in the following litany:

One: Listen to the angels say, "Do not be afraid!"

Many: God is with me and will walk with me through the process.

[Allow time for silence.]

One: Listen to the angels say, "Do not be afraid!"

Many: God is with us and will walk with us through the process.

[Allow time for silence.]

One: God will not leave us nor forsake us.

Many: Even though we fear where God may lead, we know God will not leave us and God will go with us.

All: God, give us courage to let go of our control. Open us up to Christ's presence as we seek your call for our ministry. Give us strength to face our fears. Help us see that in doing so we can live into the fullness and abundance you want for us. In Jesus' name, we pray. Amen.

Ask for Jesus to walk with you through your fears. Ask God to give you courage and strength to face them. Ask the Holy Spirit to surround and transform each of the fears into places of trust.

The circle of remembering and listening in the discernment process has been busy with collecting information and listening to the people in and around the church, including the movement of the Holy Spirit. Next the team will examine all the data with a prayerful eye.

CHAPTER SEVEN

Sorting

Introduction

IN SORTING, the past meets the future, and the identity of the church becomes clearer. In an atmosphere of prayer the discernment team sorts through recurring themes, ideas, and needs and then identifies the strengths and gifts of the church. God's longing for the future draws upon the congregation's gifts and strengths.

God gives everyone gifts for vocation. As individuals move through life, they also develop skills. However, when a person chooses an occupation or activity based solely on skills, that person usually does not feel energized. On the other hand, operating out of a gift typically creates energy in the person. For example, I have *skills* to work as a cashier and have done it in the past. When I got home from a day working, though, I was drained and dreaded going to work the next morning. I have *gifts* as a photographer. When I go out to photograph scenery, I feel energized and can't wait to do it again.

The same pattern holds true for congregations. Each congregation possesses gifts that will energize the members and ministries for which they have a passion. The same congregation may have a variety of skills, but if they follow the skills alone, they will struggle to find energy for the work. God is not calling a congregation to tasks. God is calling the congregation to grow into their collective gifts.

Pondering

Before sorting information, naming gifts, and identifying themes, though, take time to rest with the information already gathered and to pay attention to the

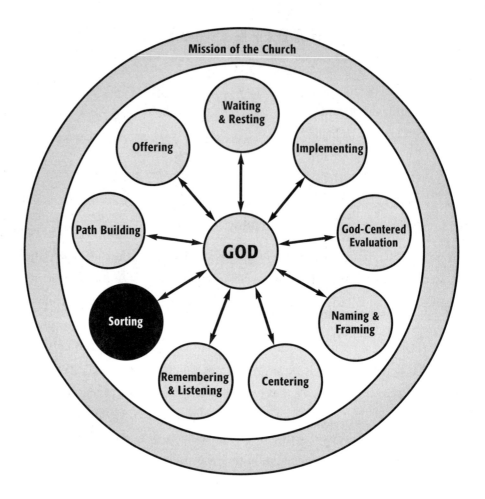

wind of the Spirit. The words in Luke 2:19, "But Mary treasured all these words and pondered them in her heart," provide good direction for holding and sorting all the information that has been gathered. Pondering allows time and space for the information to sink in and for the movement of the Holy Spirit. Do not rush this portion of the process because it can bring forth critical insights and bring the most useful information to the surface. Pondering will be more successful when each member receives a copy of all the written documentation available:

1. categorized issues, named and framed with questions
2. visions as discussed at the beginning of the process
3. the time line of the church
4. notes from listening sessions

5. community listening reports

6. insights from discussion of your mission statement(s)

7. anything else already gathered

Pondering the documentation and including the information in daily prayer allows new areas to be highlighted. Listening, pondering, and allowing room for the Holy Spirit to direct attention *is* the process. During this time, the team may want to connect through table fellowship only or for a Communion service. Allow two weeks or so (depending on your team) for this pondering before the sorting.

Sorting

Initiate the sorting process with a discussion of findings from the listening sessions. It may be helpful to post the newsprint sheets with notes and summaries. Tape the time line of the church (see page 70) on a wall if possible. Then add the information from the listening sessions at the appropriate points along the time line.

Reporting and Beginning to Process the Listening Sessions

• Who was there? / Who was missing?

• What did you hear?

• Were the messages expected? What was unexpected?

• What was omitted?

• Describe the atmosphere. For example, positive; angry; frustrated; supportive; hopeful; grieving; other

Next add findings from the community leader interviews. The team can discuss how all this information comes together and will begin to see what comments occur frequently. This is not yet a time for judgment or critique; just focus on sorting and arranging.

Common Themes

- Begin the process with prayer as always. Ask God to open eyes and ears to what has been heard. Ask for the openness to see without being critical. Include the needs you see in the church and the community.

- Looking over the data that has been gathered, what themes continue to surface?

- What needs have been mentioned by both church members and community leaders?

- What themes have surfaced in each person's prayer life and in other avenues of the Holy Spirit?

- Categorize the themes. That is, organize them into groups.

- Categorize the needs.

- How do these groups of themes and needs relate to the challenges and visions identified in chapter 4's exercises?

Once the themes and needs have been categorized, the team can devote some time to silent meditation on them before proceeding to the next exercise. Encourage each person to consider what he or she sees and feels.

Feelings

By this time the Holy Spirit has been prompting feelings. Ask the team the following questions:

Based on the movement of the Holy Spirit,

- What themes/ideas/needs bring comfort?

Bring these reflections to the large group for discussion; keep the notes for use in the next circle—Path Building.

Strengths and Gifts

After the themes and needs have been identified, the team moves on to examine the strengths and gifts in the congregation. God calls us to work out of our strengths and gifts, so review the data once again, this time looking for strengths and gifts to create another set of findings. Where does the team see the strengths of their church? What are the gifts given by God to this particular congregation?

Energy and Passion

The final set of categories in sorting will identify the energy and passion in the congregation.

Notice where the congregation spends energy in activities and ministries. Where do people receive their greatest satisfaction? What activities and ministries have drawn the most participants? What topics in team discussions have generated the most positive energy?

Energy and Passion

Ask the team the following questions:

• Where is the church's energy?

• What generates the most discussion?

• What are the issues that stand behind / underneath these discussions?

• When the church is asked to do something, which requests generate the most energy?

• What topics in team discussions have generated the most positive energy?

Sorting the information that has been gathered is a significant component of the discernment process. The church's identity, gifts, strengths, and passions will be used to build the paths of God's yearning in the next chapter.

CHAPTER EIGHT

Path Building

Introduction

IN PATH BUILDING the team explores more directly the question *What is God calling us to do?* Path building involves claiming gifts and using them for God's mission in the world. In this movement of the discernment process, the identified themes, ideas, gifts, and needs come together to form paths based on the identity and strengths of the church. These paths become the avenues along which a church actively lives into God's call.

Creativity and Imagination

In this circle the group lets its imagination loose. The team can dream as widely as possible and not discount anything. The Holy Spirit works through imagination. Celia Hahn comments that "our yearning for meaning naturally draws us to our imagination for resources not available through 'hard data' or logic."[1] The energy flows in two directions as the Holy Spirit invites daring visions, and the visions open the discernment team to the movement of the Spirit. The use of the arts (photography, drawing, music, dance) allows the group to envision even larger possibilities.

Discernment involves thinking outside the box and encouraging ideas that normally would be dismissed as impossible to rise to the surface. Howard Friend puts it this way:

> When you need gasoline for the mower, you arrive at the service station with a five-gallon can. When you walk to a neighbor's to borrow some sugar, you knock with a cup in your hand. So when Nicodemus confronted Jesus that night [John 3], he arrived with an "answer-shaped container" to carry home Jesus' reply. He may have expected new thoughts—but Jesus spoke instead of a new way of thinking.[2]

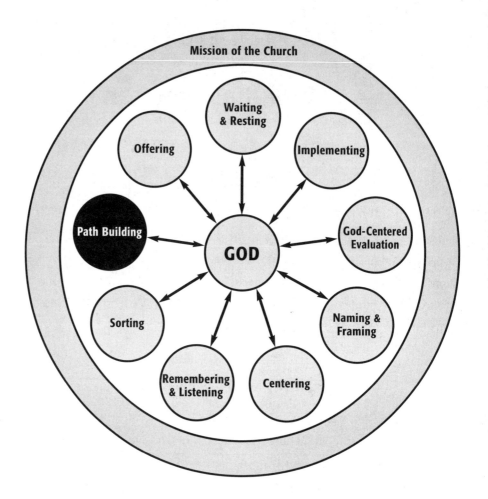

It is part of our human nature to bring "answer-shaped containers" to the discernment process. However, we need to be aware of them in the same way we attune ourselves to the fears we bring to the table. Team members are called upon to open their hearts, minds, and souls to the new ways of thinking where the Holy Spirit is leading. As the team becomes creative, God will shape the container and form the paths the team will explore.

God's Call

Path building leads toward the final answers to your discernment question. In this circle of the discernment process the team will work on ideas based on all the information that has been gathered. After naming possible paths, the group will determine which ones seem to draw the church closer to God and then begin refining those. At this point in the process all of the task-oriented, strategic-plan-oriented members of the team feel more comfortable because something concrete is finally happening. However, keep in mind that building the paths in discernment differs from strategic planning by virtue of the time spent listening to God before moving to the action component.

Focusing on the identity of the church continues to be a foundation in path building. God calls a church into mission based on who it is, not what every other church is doing. "Renewal from within requires a clear sense of self-identity. . . . 'First we must know who we *are*, and then we will know what to do.'"[3] The team should take time to retrieve information already gathered about the church's identity.

Identity

Review the following exercises you've completed previously. Notice, gather, and record on newsprint the most significant points from your earlier summaries.

- The Church As a Person—chapter 3
- Strengths and Gifts—chapter 7
- Energy and Passion—chapter 7

The first step in path building is to think in broad terms with the Holy Spirit as your guide. Where does it seem God is leading the church? For example:

- God is calling this church to remain an urban church and provide ministry to the community around it.
- God is calling this church to serve older generations.
- God is calling this church to a ministry of contemplation.
- God is calling this church to a ministry of mentoring young adults.
- God is calling this church to . . .

Other areas of exploration might be:
- God is calling forth leaders in the church to do . . .
- God is calling the church to use its facilities for . . .
- God is calling the church to use its finances for . . .

Most of the time the discernment team will list more than one area to which they feel God is calling the church. At this stage it is important to pursue each one of the options. All the possibilities need to be explored now. And, God's yearning for the church may be made up of several similar paths. In other words, these paths are the possible directions God desires for the mission of the church. Specifics for each path will be discussed later.

Where Are the Paths Leading?

Gather the results from all the exercises, especially those in chapter 7, and have them available for reference.

Prayer Time
- Spend at least fifteen minutes in prayer and meditation.
    ~ Individuals who are comfortable with silence can go out of the room and meditate for the designated time period.
    ~ Individuals who need to process verbally can stay in the room and talk prayerfully with each other. Be clear that these individuals are not making decisions. They are listening to the Spirit in conversation.
- Ask each person to meditate on the question *Based on the all the information we have, along what path would Jesus take this church?*

Coming Together
- Report back what was heard in the prayer time.
    ~ *If Jesus were setting the direction for our church, where would it go?*
- Record the feedback on newsprint.
- What patterns emerge?
- In which directions does it appear that God is calling us? (Probably there will be more than one direction.)

Building the Paths

Having named possible paths, the discernment team can start constructing the paths. For example, if God is calling the church to ministry with older generations, what might that look like? Generate pertinent questions such as: *Whom would this ministry serve? What picture do the demographics present? What are the needs of these people? What programs would meet the needs?*

The team will take each direction identified and explore how to build a path to get there. The group will want to go back and look at ideas that were uncovered as they worked through the process. Follow the exercise below for each possible path. If something seems impossible, don't stop. Continue through the exercise. Remember, God's vision is bigger than ours.

Path Name _____

Working in a large group or in small groups, discuss the following questions:

- It seems at this time that God may be calling this church to
  (describe a direction)

- What themes characterize this path?

- Who are the possible leaders from the church for this path?

- How does this path serve God?

- What changes would we need to make as a church to take this path?

Satellite View

Building the paths focuses on the how-tos. After the exercise to build all possible paths is done, the group can step back and look at the whole picture. In the language of today, it is time to get the satellite view of the paths. The following two exercises enable the team to envision the paths as they connect to one another and the church.

The Paths in Relationship to Each Other
• Which paths are similar and how?

• Which paths are different and how?

• How do you feel about each path? List your fears, joys, and concerns.

A Satellite View
Relationships (both within the church and with the community)
Look at each path and respond to these questions:
• Who would benefit from the church taking this path?
• Would anyone be injured if the church takes this path?

Connections
Refer to the drawing of the church as a body.
• Replicate the drawing.
• Add the possible paths on the drawing in different colors.
• How do the paths fit into the identity of the church?
• Are there any paths that stand out?
• Which paths are connected?
• Do any paths seem out of place for this body?

From looking at the paths in relationship to the church and to the community, the team now considers how each path relates to God. In the next four circles of the discernment process, the paths are examined through various lenses, and changes are made as God leads. These final circles flow together with a lot of movement back and forth among them. And yet each one has a distinctive purpose.

CHAPTER NINE

Offering

Introduction

EARLIER IN THE WORKBOOK we mentioned the propensity of many churches to develop an idea, direction, or program, and then ask God to bless it. In this circle, the team offers the paths to God and continues communication with God. The question of this circle, *God, what do you think?* encourages the team to discern which paths connect with God's longing for the church. The team gives the Holy Spirit time to stir the feelings regarding the paths toward either desolation or consolation.

The Paths and Their Relationship with God

Several paths may be possible for the church, so looking at them from a different perspective is key to making choices. Spiritual discernment is about seeking God's yearning for the church. If this is the case, then the paths chosen should bring the church, its members, and those with whom the church interacts closer to God.

There are several activities to choose from in this chapter. Each provides a different way to hear God's leading. These exercises provide an alternative to voting; however, they require team members to pay close attention to God's guidance. The activities also allow the different personality types in your group to sense the paths and their relationships with God. Be sensitive to what team members are saying and feeling. No matter which exercises you choose, conclude with "The Offering" at the end of the chapter.

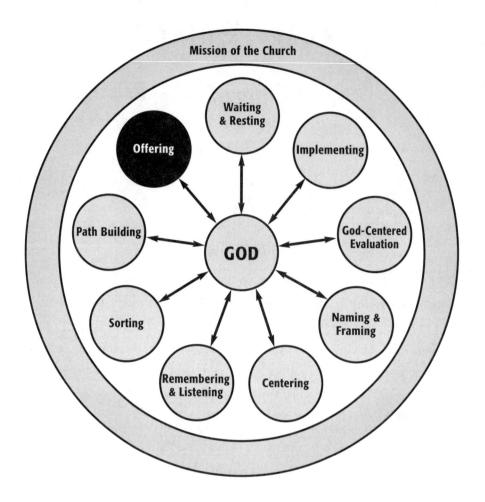

It is time to ask questions that link the church and God for each possible path. *Does this path move the church and all those involved nearer to God or further away? Is it a path that keeps the church centered on Christ?* The choices the team has identified and described should lead the church into a deeper relationship with God. Possible paths may be uncomfortable because they lead the church in new directions, and yet those directions may meet the ultimate goal of drawing closer to God continually.

Relationship with God

Look at each possible path and answer the following questions:
- How does this path move the church, its members, and all those served closer to God?

- How does this path move the church, its members, and all those served further away from God?

Where Is the Holy Spirit Leading?

Take time again to pause and step back to gain perspective. Allow the soul of each individual in the group to catch up with the Holy Spirit. The group needs to let go of control and let the Spirit indicate the path God would have the church take. Think of the Spirit as the primary actor now, while the discernment team becomes the audience. Letting go of control is scary, so think about trust. The team and all its individual members need to

- trust the Holy Spirit to be involved;
- trust the process to bring forth insight;
- trust that God wants abundance for the church;
- trust that God's yearning is toward wholeness–shalom.

Such a level of trust asks that the team let go of its fears and its need for control. The process of spiritual discernment is not about each person or about the church. Ultimately it is about how God can use the church to advance God's mission in the world. The ability of the team members to rely on God alone, expecting that God will provide abundance for the church, calls upon each member to have a faith centered in experiences of God's trustworthiness.

Letting Go
List the areas where the team members are having a hard time trusting the Holy Spirit.

If the group is struggling with trust, go back to chapter 3 and the images for God that guide the group in meetings. Name the images or explore biblical stories that will help build trust for God's leadership through the final circles in the process.

Lift up in prayer the areas where trust is difficult.

Read over the information on all the paths. Which ones generate more energy among the team members? The paths will need to be adapted and expanded, but which ones seem to have the light of Christ shining on them?

Remember, there is no one right path, and usually there is not 100 percent clarity. God does not ask humans to be right but to be honest and faithful. The team may feel God's yearning could lead down more than one path, and that is okay. Many churches have multifaceted ministries, and God is often working on multiple options.

Guided Meditation

In order to identify areas of comfort, areas of challenge, and areas of difficulty among the paths, use the following guided meditation in a group setting, and then discuss what members of the team felt and learned.

Close your eyes and take three deep breaths. In your mind, go to your favorite safe place. Look around you, enjoying the familiar view. Savor the sense of safety and comfort.

Now look out over the landscape in front of you and see the paths you have opened up for the church. Choose the path that seems best to you today, and start walking down it. Note the activities associated with the path and the people who are with you. Let the scene change moment by moment. Allow Jesus to walk the path with you to see how it feels. Listen to what Jesus says to you about this path for the church.

When you and Jesus have finished your conversation, allow yourself a few moments just to breathe. Then slowly open your eyes and return to the room. Write down your reflections about this path.

At this stage, if the paths are quite clear, the discernment team may go on to the next section on consolation and desolation. However, if differences of opinion persist, and the group has not identified the path or paths the church is exploring, then the next exercise will help the group sort out their feelings.

To Which Paths Does the Holy Spirit Point?

Take time for personal prayer and meditation. Invite each person to ask God to clear away the fog so that the group can see where the Spirit is resting.

Listen carefully to one another as the group responds to the following questions. Often disagreement results when people have misunderstood each other or when some people feel they have not been heard.

- What places on each path feel uncomfortable?
- How does each path need to be adapted?

If the group is still struggling because no path is clear or there are differences of opinion, move back to both of the following circles:

- the centering circle; revisit core values and holy indifference.
- the path building circle; start the process again.

Consolation or Desolation
(or Confusion in the Middle)

When a path or set of paths has risen to the surface, test the group's feeling about the decision. Saint Ignatius of Loyola described this step in discernment as naming a feeling of either *consolation* or *desolation*. Do the paths that are rising to the level of affirmation bring consolation (a sense of moving closer to God) or desolation (a sense of being separated from God)? In other words, if the decision is of God, hearts will be consoled with feelings of joy, tranquility, peace, and trust. If the decision is not of God, there will be an uneasy feeling, a heaviness of heart, or a sense of weight on the shoulders of the team members. We have added a third option: confusion in the middle—neither fully consolation nor fully desolation.

If the designated paths bring consolation, identify what feels good about them. Perhaps one or more of the paths are clear. However, there may be a new, risky path for the church. That path may bring both consolation and fear because it means stepping out into the unknown, and that is okay. Recall that whenever the angels appear, they say, "Do not be afraid." Let the angels bring courage as the church faces a new path full of God's yearning, even though that path may also be full of fear and uncertainty.

Consolation

Consider each possible path for the church one at a time, using these questions for reflection.

• Does this path bring consolation?

• Does this path bring the church closer to who God is calling it to be?

• What feels good about it?

• Name the fears connected to this path. Where does the team need to hear the angels say, "Do not be afraid"?

If any of the paths under consideration are bringing desolation, ask what feels uncomfortable about the path and why? Is the desolation due to fear of the unknown or an uncertain future? If so, examine the fear. Is the fear due to God's asking the church to do something people always believed it would never do? If this is the case, then the path may indeed be a good and right one, and the team needs to go back to chapter 5 and re-read the section on holy indifference.

However, if the fear and desolation arise because the path "just doesn't feel right," listen to that intuition, for it may be the Holy Spirit speaking. Go back over the process to see what has been missed or forgotten. Go back also if the team answers "both" to the question *Does the path bring consolation or desolation?*

If a path clearly rises to the top and brings consolation and a sense of excitement to the team, it is appropriate to offer it up to God once again. In Acts 15 the disciples and others met for what is called the Jerusalem Council to make decisions regarding the future of the early Christian communities. In verse 28, Peter speaks regarding one of the decisions: "It has seemed good to the Holy Spirit and to us," and then he goes on to share the decision. Now that the team has uncovered the path or paths God is calling them to take, those paths can be offered to God in this same way.

It has seemed good to the Holy Spirit and to us.

—Acts 15:28

The Offering
Write a short description of each path that the group can use in the following prayer:

Loving God, who calls us beloved and names us as children, we offer this path up to you. It feels good to the Holy Spirit and to us that this church

_____.

(Name of the Path)

We pray your blessings on this path, in the name of Jesus, who has been our companion on the journey. Amen.

Now that the team has offered the paths to God, it is time to wait and rest. In the next circle the team will allow the offering to be with God for transformation before beginning to implement any plans.

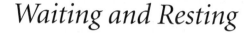

CHAPTER TEN

Waiting and Resting

Introduction

THE KEY WORD for this chapter is *wait*. So often groups make decisions and then jump right into the activities required to bring the decision to life. Society teaches us that once a decision is made, we are to act on it. To do anything else means the group is not decisive, or that it can envision but not bring the vision to fruition. Immediate action is the way of the world. Romans 12:2 says, "Do not be conformed to this world." As Christians we are to be countercultural, and that includes this stage of the discernment process. The paths have just been offered to God, and now it is time to wait and rest with God before implementing these paths.

The team needs to live with the results of the discernment process for a while. Once again, the team steps back, rests, and gains some perspective. Occasionally churches step into the process and find out too late that time casts a new light on the paths. It is often a light that was blocked by the discernment team in the midst of intense consideration of the paths. So wait, let go, gauge feelings, and modify the paths as needed.

Resting

The team has given the paths to God as an offering. Let God transform them. While the team is resting, it might be a good time to reflect on the process.

Reflection
Spend some time reflecting on what has been done throughout the discernment process. Use the following questions to help summarize what the group has learned and felt.

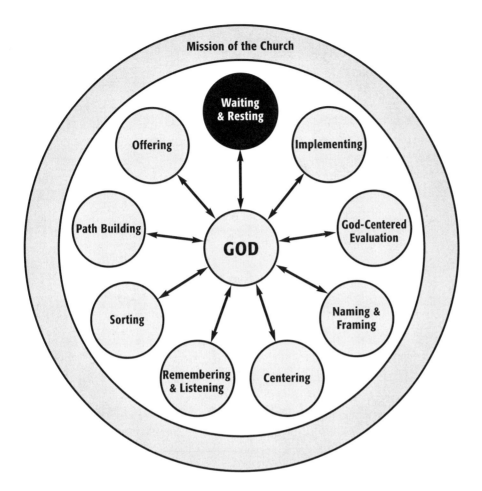

- When was God's presence felt?

- When did it feel as if God was absent and why?

- What new learning or relationship do you have with God?

During this period of resting, regular prayer and Bible study can keep the team in touch with one another and with God's continual leading. Celebrating sabbath dinners together on Friday evenings provides another way to remain in contact. Here are a few ideas for making the most of sabbath dinners:

- Talk about how individual team members have seen their faith grow.
- Explore, at a deeper level, stories in the Bible that resonated with team members during the process.
- Pray together.
- Laugh and enjoy one another's company.
- Refer to the books on sabbath, such as

  Reinventing Sunday by Brad Berglund

  Sabbath by Wayne Muller

  Sabbath Time by Tilden Edwards

Corrective Action

After a period of resting (a month or longer) the discernment team should meet to see how everyone is feeling. How has the Spirit moved within each person? What feelings have come to the surface? What corrective action needs to be taken?

Corrective Action

Ask the group the following questions:

- How are you feeling about the paths?

- Where are the feelings coming from?

- What corrective actions need to be taken now?

Only by continuing to pay attention to the movement of the Holy Spirit will the team be able to develop new paths. Of course, it is always easier to correct the direction of a path earlier in the process rather than later. Now that the team has let the paths rest in God for transformation and corrective action, it can move into implementation.

CHAPTER ELEVEN

Implementing

Introduction

THE TIME HAS COME to put the paths into action. A lot of time has been spent discerning God's yearning for the future of the church. The church can now start living into its future. Changes have been taking place in the church as the process has unfolded. This circle focuses on the details of the path implementation and communication with the entire congregation.

Implementing what was uncovered in the discernment process is similar to and different from implementing any plan. It is similar in that the tasks are outlined, people are chosen to carry out the tasks, and action is taken. It is different in that God continues to be the focus of all the work.

Beginning Stages of Implementation

While the discernment team will not necessarily be the group to develop the paths leading the church, the team does need to give some thought to the process. Most likely the answers to the following questions have already emerged. Take time to put them together. Gather all the path-building sheets developed from the questions on page 93 with adaptations you have made to them. These sheets will provide the core for implementation.

(NAME OF THE PATH)

Begin with prayer:
Loving God who has led us through this process, remind us that you want to be in the implementation as much as you want us to discern your mind. Keep us open to your leading. Help us to hold our planning

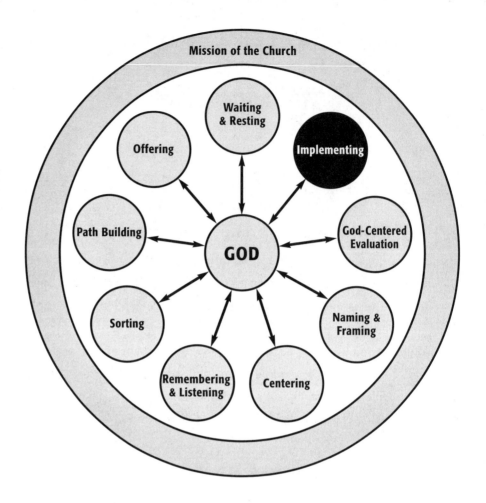

Mission of the Church

- Waiting & Resting
- Offering
- Implementing
- Path Building
- GOD
- God-Centered Evaluation
- Sorting
- Naming & Framing
- Remembering & Listening
- Centering

lightly so as not to take control back from you. Give us wisdom, give us courage, and give us strength for this leg of the journey. In Jesus' name, we pray. Amen.

Who has God raised up to be on the leadership team for this path?

With the Holy Spirit as your guide, name the steps to implement this path as far as possible with room to shift and grow.

Choosing a team of leaders for each path is necessary. The discernment team talked about possible leaders in the path-building circle and in the previous exercise. Prayerfully consider the individuals already identified and whether the Spirit is still lifting them up. If so, ask them to take on leadership roles. If the discernment team feels led to reconsider leadership, or someone declines the invitation, don't get discouraged. Pay attention to the people God is putting in your path. Also understand that the "right" person for the job may not be clear at this point; if that is the case, move onto the other paths or continue praying.

The leaders for each path form a *lead team*; this team joins the discernment team for the implementation of the paths. Share with the new leaders the paths God has raised to the surface. Encourage these leaders to continue the work in a prayerful manner. Ask them to read through this book, so they may have an idea of how to continue listening to God in their work. We recommend the new team spend time especially with the first three chapters as they begin to build a foundation and work together.

Take things slowly so that everyone can catch up with all the work that has been done. Moving slowly also allows for continued listening to the Holy Spirit and to one another. Don't be alarmed if everything doesn't fall into place immediately. Even though the team has made a decision, God may still be putting things into place. Be patient and don't rush what can't be rushed.

Sharing with the Congregation

The discernment team needs to communicate the paths to the congregation. Although the team has been giving updates throughout the process, a final report opens the paths to everyone. The reporting takes the form of a worship service. Everyone can participate in a celebration of thanksgiving.

CHAPTER 12

God-Centered Evaluation

THE LEAD TEAM and the discernment team need to continue to listen to God and to evaluate what is happening in the life of the church, being attentive to how the church stays on the path(s) God has opened up before them. Discernment is never done. Listening, remembering, waiting, praying, and taking corrective actions continue as long as the church is active. The intensity of these practices may change as the church moves forward along the paths. A range of evaluation techniques may be used, but these techniques are nuanced by continually listening to God. The lead team and the discernment team want to be alert for new ideas and the nudging of the Holy Spirit.

The discernment team stays active as a group that is removed from the implementation of actions. Ronald Heifetz calls this "getting up on the balcony."[1] This perspective allows the team to reflect without being immersed in the immediacy of daily activity. Working from the balcony will make it easier for team members to listen to God, since they will not be in the middle of the action. The lead team, in the middle of the process, listens to what people are saying about problems and stories of success.

We suggest that the two teams meet on a regular basis for sharing and praying while paying attention to the rhythms of discernment and to the places where God comes alongside them. Meetings with both groups could be based around questions such as the following:

- Where have we seen God active in the implementation?
- What is the general mood of the congregation?
- Where are people encountering difficulty?

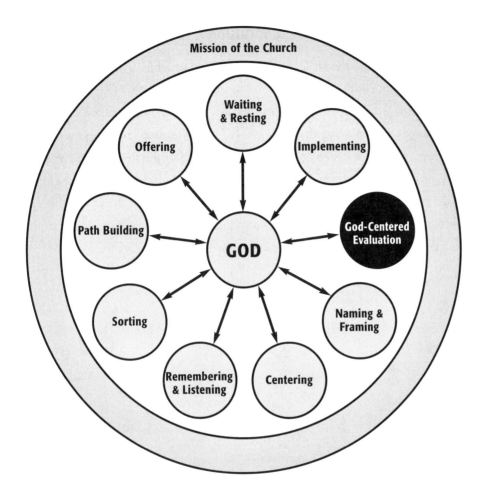

- After prayer, ask whether the difficulty may be the result of leaving God out of the implementation.
- What needs to be celebrated? For what shall you give thanks to God?

When asking these questions, make sure to continue the practices of silence, attentive listening, and prayer.

The discernment team is encouraged to continue discernment in their personal lives. If they have not already done so, it is appropriate to work through the personal discernment workbook *Living into the Answers: A Workbook for Personal Spiritual Discernment*. Some churches have found that the team's enthusiasm about discernment is contagious, and others want to learn the practice.

Conclusion

The discernment process is filled with prayer and worship, with discussion and interaction, with addressing issues and facing the challenges of congregational life. Implementation of the paths starts the discernment process again. Celebrating the changes and entering the new paths of God's leading enhance the energy and passion of the whole congregation. And the primary question always remains: *God, what is your yearning for our church?* The new paths lead the church closer to the relationship God longs for. The new paths also become the ways of listening for God's leading. Discernment continues to be an interactive and dynamic process that opens the church up to transformation and new life.

APPENDIX A

Worshipful-Work® Ideas

Agenda

Design a meeting's agenda to look like an order of worship.

- Light candle(s) to represent Christ's light shining on the meeting.
- Include confession of corporate sin (for example, weariness, frustration, confusion).
- Committee reports can be the offering.
- Include litanies of thanksgiving after reports.
    - ~Say together, "We give you thanks, O Lord" after reports.
    - ~Sing a hymn of thanksgiving such as "Now Thank We All Our God."
- Include planned hymns.
- Proclamation of the Word can be a biblical story with reflection that enlightens items on the agenda.
- Celebrate the Lord's Supper.

Prayer

- Opening prayer is a reminder of God's presence and interest in the business.
- Closing prayer is an offertory for the work done and a request for assistance in "letting go" of the business.
- Allow for prayer during meetings. Assign four people to keep their eyes and ears open for specific matters for prayer. At the end of the meeting their observations are built into closing worship/prayers:
    - ~prayers of thanksgiving for God's blessings
    - ~prayers of intercession for the church and the world
    - ~prayers of petition for the needs of the board/committee
    - ~prayers of praise for the work of the Holy Spirit in the life of the church

- Ongoing prayer: invite individuals to pray silently for each member of the group and the business at hand. Here are two possible methods:
  - ~ Assign individuals to specific fifteen-minute segments of the meeting.
  - ~ Pass a candle around the table. Whoever has the candle is the designated "pray-er."
- Time out for prayer. When discussion becomes heated or bogged down, take three to five minutes for silent personal prayer to let go and refocus on God. Individuals can consider the following questions:[1]
  - ~ Am I closing myself off from information we need to make this decision?
  - ~ Whom do I need to forgive to be more fully present?
  - ~ What is an image of God that needs to come to bear in this setting?
  - ~ How does the scripture we read shed light on us now?
  - ~ Am I operating in a need-to-win or need-to-save-face mode?
  - ~ How would servant leaders make this decision?
  - ~ How am I blocking the work of the Holy Spirit?
- Take time for prayer or silence when creativity is needed.
- Agree on what the group will pray about before the next meeting.

Discussion
- Train board members in attentive listening.
- Allow for times of silence so introverts have time to reflect and share.
- Utilize a speaking stick (or other object). Only the person holding the object can speak.

Music
- Play meditative music as the group is gathering.
- Provide a songbook for each person.
- Stop to sing Taizé or other prayerful, centering music when it fits the business at hand.

Reflection
- Take time for reflection on what is happening during the meeting.
- Build in time for reflection at the end of the meeting to ensure all voices have been heard.

Leadership

- Designate a spiritual guide or director for the meeting. This person will listen for occasions to
  - ~stop for prayer;
  - ~sing a song;
  - ~tell a biblical story;
  - ~bring the group back to center in Christ;
  - ~listen for those who haven't spoken.

Sacred Space

- Create a warm, welcoming environment by softening the meeting space decor (consider, for example, lighting, seating, room arrangement).
- Place meditative art work around the room and in the hallway leading to the meeting space.
- Use a colorful woven cloth or liturgical cloth on the table.

APPENDIX B

Images for God

Exercise 1   Current Images for God[1]

When I pray, I imagine God as: *(Describe or draw your image.)*

I am comfortable/uncomfortable with many images for God because:

How have my images for God changed during my lifetime?

How do I experience God/Jesus/the Holy Spirit now?

How would I describe the ways God/Jesus/the Holy Spirit relates to me?

Exercise 2   Biblical Images for God[2]

Look at the following biblical passages and write down the images for God.

Scripture	God is like (description)	God's activities (verbs)
2 Samuel 22:2-4	a rock, fortress	one who delivers, saves
Psalm 123:2		
Isaiah 64:8		

Scripture	God is like (description)	God's activities (verbs)
Genesis 3:21		
Hosea 13:7-8		
Luke 12:27-28		
Luke 13:34		
Job 10:8-12		
Deuteronomy 32:11-12		
John 3:3-7		

How do these images affect my ability to trust God?

What new images might help me as I enter a process of spiritual discernment?

Exercise 3   EXPERIENCING GOD[3]

As you consider your images for God, recall ways you have experienced God in your lifetime. List about ten adjectives that describe God (such as, eternal, kind, powerful, loving, judging, distant, personal, etc.).

Now choose three of the adjectives and write a paragraph for each that describes times when your experience of God matched that adjective. For example, if you chose *loving*, *distant*, and *powerful*, start by writing about an experience of a loving God that you remember. Do the same for the other two words.

Now, remember what you were taught about God as a child. How does that teaching match or differ from your own experiences of God?

Ask another person to do this exercise. Then share your list and experiences with that person, listening for similarities and differences. Talk about how you each understand the ways God has been involved in your life.

Finally, note how your relationship with God has changed with the different experiences. Recall any biblical images for God that match your own experiences.

Exercise 4   **SENSING GOD**[4]

In this exercise identify how you sense God in different settings.

1. When I have experienced a loss, I sense God . . .

2. When my back is against the wall, I sense God . . .

3. When I see a rainbow, I sense God . . .

4. When I make a mistake, I sense God . . .

5. When I am quiet, I sense God . . .

6. When something unexpected happens, I sense God . . .

7. When I hear a special piece of music, I sense God . . .

Look over your sentences, and notice anything that surprises you. Has your understanding of God (or yourself) changed as you have completed these four exercises?

APPENDIX C

Spiritual Practices

Meditation

Meditation is a spiritual practice that allows the Holy Spirit to speak through prayerful thought on a reading or subject. A biblical text often serves as the basis of meditation. A portion of scripture is read and then time follows to think about what the words are saying to the reader today. Thoughts are then recorded. Meditation on scripture rather than reading commentaries or devotional materials allows the Bible to speak to the reader. The question is asked, *What is God saying to me in this text today?*

In the discernment process, the Bible is read with an eye on the primary questions. Another way of asking the question is, *How is this text speaking to my church and to our discernment process?* It is helpful if everyone on the discernment team reads the same biblical text every day.

Suggested texts are:

- The daily Lectionary, available at http://divinity.lib.vanderbilt.edu /lectionary or at your denomination's Web site. The daily Lectionary will include Old Testament and New Testament readings, a psalm, and a passage from one of the New Testament letters. You may want to decide which of these you will read.
- A good selection of scripture would include one psalm and a small portion of one of the Gospels. The Gospels could be read in this order— Mark, Luke, Matthew, and John.

Members of the discernment team are asked to record their thoughts so that they may refer to them throughout the discernment process. Each person may want to start a discernment journal (refer to chapter 3 and the section on journaling).

Lectio Divina with a Group

Lectio divina is a way of reading the Bible that has been practiced in the Roman Catholic Church for centuries. Assuming that God is continually reaching out to humankind in order to be in relationship, there needs to be a process for listening. One good way to listen is by hearing a portion of the scripture read again and again. In *lectio divina* the rhythm of listening is made up of movement into and out of the biblical text. The movement has four parts, each represented by a Latin word.

Lectio:	reading, paying attention
Meditatio:	thinking about the passage, letting it sink in to feeling, to the heart
Oratio:	praying, simply and briefly
Contemplatio:	being with God in the silence

Choose a portion of scripture (or the mission statement of the church). The process works best when various scripture passages are used over time. The Lectionary texts provide a good method to focus on a variety of scripture passages.

Find comfortable places to sit and begin in silence, paying attention to the rhythm of breathing.

Lectio
Have one person read the scripture aloud. Listen for a word or phrase that strikes you. Have another person read it again, and see if your mind stays on the same word or phrase. After a few minutes of silence, share your words or phrases.

Meditatio
In silence think about the word or phrase that struck you. Let it sink into your heart. What are you feeling about it? What does it mean to you? Write down your thoughts and feelings. Spend some time sharing your thoughts with the group.

Oratio

Have a third person read the passage aloud again. Form your thoughts and feelings into a one-sentence prayer. Speak your sentence prayer aloud, lifting your thoughts and feelings to the Lord and asking for healing, fullness, or insight. When the sentence prayers have been spoken, move into silence.

Contemplatio

Sit in silence for at least three minutes, opening yourself up to the triune Presence. If your mind wanders, bring it back with your word or phrase. Focus on being open and listening. End this time of silence with a focus on breathing. Share your experience with the group.

APPENDIX D

Service of Transition

WE GATHER IN GOD'S NAME

Gather in Silence

Welcome

*Opening Song	"Come to Us"	*Upper Room Worshipbook,* #55

*Prayer

Gracious God, as darkness draws this day to a close, we remember with thanksgiving the gifts you have given us and the signs of your blessings. O Christ, there is the miracle of your mysterious and compassionate presence among us.[1] O Spirit of the Living God, as we enter worship, give us words for those unspoken prayers in our hearts. Thanks be to God. Amen.

THANKSGIVING FOR THE MOTHERS AND FATHERS OF OUR FAITH

Scripture	Hebrews 12:1	
Sung Response	"O Lord, Hear My Prayer," stanza 1	*Music of Taizé*

Litany of Remembrance

One: Eternal and Almighty God, we give you thanks for all the faithful people who have gone before us.

Many: For the great cloud of witnesses in the Bible like Abraham and Sarah, Moses and Miriam, Joseph and Mary, Priscilla and Aquila.

One: We give you thanks for the great cloud of witnesses who have gone before us in this faith community.

Many: We remember stories from the past, telling us of the work others have done on your behalf.

One:	Inspire us to follow in their footsteps and to be faithful disciples of Christ.
All:	Let us remember all those who have been a part of our faith journeys with thanksgiving and praise.

Silence

ACKNOWLEDGING THE EMPTINESS OF LOSS

Scripture   Psalm 13:1-2

Sung Response   "O Lord, Hear My Prayer," stanza 1

Litany of Loss

One:	Comforting One and Compassionate One, whose healing presence knows no boundaries,
Many:	Be with us all as we remember those who have left, as we suffer loss, and experience the ache and pain of grieving.[2]
One:	God of eternity, many have come and many have gone within this congregation.
Many:	We understand their leaving, and yet we also feel the empty space they left behind—an emptiness in our hearts and souls.
One:	O God who stands with us for all time,
Many:	We are grateful for the journey we shared with the ones who have left. Yet, we miss those who deepened our joy and lightened our sorrow.[3] We miss their friendship and companionship. We miss their leadership and compassion.
One:	God of Steadfast Love,
Many:	Bring comfort into the emptiness. Touch our memories with grace and peace.
All:	Amen and Amen.

Silence

OUR RESPONSE

Scripture   1 Samuel 7:12

Silent Offering of Names   (Participants write names of those they miss on slips of paper and place them on the Communion table as they are ready. They take a polished stone from the table as a reminder that God is always with them.)

WE COME TO THE TABLE OF HEALING AND CELEBRATION

Words of Institution

The Bread and the Cup

WE LOOK FORWARD TO A NEW DAY

Scripture   Acts 11:23-26

Litany of Celebration

One: God of life, we give you thanks for this church and all who have been part of it in the past.

Many: The stories of those who have left will always be a part of us, and we will carry them with us as we move into a new day.

One: We thank you for the gifts we will receive as we welcome new members into the story of this church and our lives.

Many: Open our hearts and minds so that we may welcome them into our family. Help us to be receptive to new ideas, new relationships, and new workers.

One: God whose love knows no boundaries,

Many: We look forward to the newness that is around the bend.

All: Triune God, with your help we will continue to be a faith community in this place for a long time. Hallelujah! Praise the Lord! Amen.

*Closing Hymn   "God of Day and God of Darkness," stanzas 1, 3, 4
                      Upper Room Worshipbook, #201

*The Blessing
Holy and loving God, reconcile, renew, and restore us by our grace through Jesus Christ, that we may rest in peace this night. Amen.

Leave in silence

*Stand as you are able

Notes on the service:
The service is best done in the evening or at twilight. Have candles or oil lamps burning before participants arrive. Print prayers or thoughts for meditation on the inside cover of the bulletin. As people gather, during the offering of names, and during Communion, quiet meditative music can be played. The slips of paper with names on them can be buried after the service.

NOTES

Chapter 1

1. Celia Allison Hahn, *Uncovering Your Church's Hidden Spirit* (Bethesda, MD: Alban Institute, 2001), 87–88.

2. Charles M. Olsen, *Transforming Church Boards into Communities of Spiritual Leaders* (Bethesda, MD: Alban Institute, 1995), 10.

3. Mary Benet McKinney, *Sharing Wisdom: A Process for Group Decision Making* (Allen, TX: Thomas More Publishing, 1998), 13.

Chapter 2

1. Charles M. Olsen and Ellen Morseth, *Selecting Church Leaders: A Practice in Spiritual Discernment* (Nashville, TN: Upper Room Books, 2002), 21.

2. Ibid., 23.

Chapter 3

1. Parker Palmer in speech at the Pacific School of Religion, 1993.

2. Olsen, *Transforming Church Boards*, 8–16.

3. Ibid., 13.

4. The meanings for these Greek words come from Walter Bauer, *A Greek-English Lexicon of the New Testament*, trans. William F. Arndt and F. Wilbur Gingrich (Chicago: University of Chicago Press, 1957).

5. Simon Chan, *Spiritual Theology: A Systematic Study of the Christian Life* (Downers Grove, IL: InterVarsity Press, 1998), 213.

6. Olsen, *Transforming Church Boards*, 24.

7. Hahn, *Uncovering Your Church's Hidden Spirit*, 5.

8. Corinne Ware, *Discover Your Spiritual Type: A Guide to Individual and Congregational Growth* (Bethesda, MD: The Alban Institute, 1995), 49–52.

9. Hahn, *Uncovering Your Church's Hidden Spirit*, 62–63.

10. Janet R. Cawley, *Who Is Our Church? Imagining Congregational Identity* (Herndon, VA: Alban Institute, 2006), 60, 61–62.

11. Wendy Wright, "Passing Angels: The Art of Spiritual Discernment" (*Weavings*, November/December, 1995):10-11.

12. Stephen V. Doughty, "Mystery and Institutional Rebirth" (*Weavings*, January/February 2006):24–25.

Chapter 5

1. Wilkie W. Au and Noreen Cannon Au, *The Discerning Heart: Exploring the Christian Path* (New York: Paulist Press, 2006), 60.

2. Danny E. Morris and Charles M. Olsen, *Discerning God's Will Together: A Spiritual Practice for the Church* (Bethesda, MD: Alban Publications, 1997), 74.

3. Olsen and Morseth, *Selecting Church Leaders*, 64–65.

Chapter 6

1. Hahn, *Uncovering Your Church's Hidden Spirit*, 57.

2. Maureen Conroy, *The Discerning Heart: Discovering a Personal God* (Chicago: Loyola University Press, 1993), 15.

3. See Olsen, *Transforming Church Boards*, 64–65.

4. Olsen, *Transforming Church Boards*, 64.

5. Roy M. Oswald and Robert E. Friedrich Jr., *Discerning Your Congregation's Future: A Strategic and Spiritual Approach* (Bethesda, MD: Alban Institute, 1996), 85.

Chapter 8

1. Hahn, *Uncovering Your Church's Hidden Spirit*, 53.

2. Howard E. Friend Jr., *Recovering the Sacred Center: Church Renewal from the Inside Out* (Valley Forge, PA: Judson Press, 1998), 6–7.

3. Ibid., 4–5.

Chapter 12

1. Ronald A Heifetz and Donald L. Laurie, "The Work of Leadership," *Harvard Business Review* (January-February 1997): 125, as cited in Gil Rendle, *Behavioral Covenants in Congregations* (Baltimore, MD: Alban Institute, 1999), 41.

Appendix A

1. Based on Olsen, *Transforming Church Boards*, 22–24.

Appendix B

1. From *Living into the Answers*, 33–34.

2. From *Living into the Answers*, 34–35.

3. From *Living into the Answers*, 35–36.

4. From *Living into the Answers*, 36–37.

Appendix D

1. Elise S. Eslinger, ed., *Upper Room Worshipbook: Music and Liturgies for Spiritual Formation* (Nashville, TN: Upper Room Books, 2006), 28–29, adapted.

2. Miriam Therese Winter, *WomanWisdom: A Feminist Lectionary and Psalter, Women of the Hebrew Scriptures: Part One* (New York: Crossroad, 1991), 250, paraphrased.

3. *Book of Occasional Services: A Liturgical Resource Supplementing the Book of Worship*, 1993 (Louisville, KY: Geneva Press, 1999), 240.

BIBLIOGRAPHY

Ackerman, John. *Spiritual Awakening: A Guide to Spiritual Life in Congregations*. Bethesda, MD: Alban Institute, 1994.

Au, Wilkie, and Noreen Cannon Au. *The Discerning Heart: Exploring the Christian Path*. New York: Paulist Press, 2006.

Bass, Diana Butler. *Christianity for the Rest of Us: How the Neighborhood Church Is Transforming Faith*. New York: HarperCollins Publishers, 2007.

—————. *The Practicing Congregation: Imagining a New Old Church*. Herndon, VA: Alban Institute, 2004.

————— and Joseph Stewart-Sicking. *From Nomads to Pilgrims: Stories from Practicing Congregations*. Herndon, VA: Alban Institute, 2006.

Bauer, Walter, William F. Arndt, and F. Wilbur Gingrich. *A Greek-English Lexicon of the New Testament and Other Early Christian Literature*. Chicago: University of Chicago Press, 1979.

Berglund, Brad. *Reinventing Sunday: Breakthrough Ideas for Transforming Worship*. Valley Forge, PA: Judson Press, 2001.

Cawley, Janet R. *Who Is Our Church? Imagining Congregational Identity*. Herndon, VA: Alban Institute, 2006.

Chan, Simon. *Spiritual Theology: A Systematic Study of the Christian Life*. Downers Grove, IL: InterVarsity Press, 1998.

Conroy, Maureen. *The Discerning Heart: Discovering a Personal God*. Chicago: Loyola University Press, 1993.

Curtiss, Victoria Grace. "Discernment and Decision-Making." A paper, 2005. Available at www.pcusa.org/peaceunitypurity/resources/discernment_and_ decision_making.pdf.

—————. *Guidelines for Communal Discernment*. Louisville, KY: Presbyterian Peacemaking Program, n.d. Available at www.hudrivpres.org/upload/docs/curtiss_discernment.pdf

Doughty, Stephen V. *To Walk in Integrity: Leadership in Times of Crisis*. Nashville, TN: Upper Room Books, 2004.

—————. "Mystery and Institutional Rebirth" in *Weavings: A Journal of Christian Life*. vol. 11, no. 1 (Jan/Feb. 2006). Issue theme is "Mystery."

Duck, Ruth C. and Maren C. Tirabassi, eds. *Touch Holiness: Resources for Worship*. Cleveland: United Church Press, 1990.

Edwards, Tilden. *Sabbath Time*, rev. ed. Nashville: Upper Room Books, 2003.

Eslinger, Elise S., ed. *Upper Room Worshipbook: Music and Liturgies for Spiritual Formation*. Nashville: Upper Room Books, 2006.

Foster, Richard J. *Celebration of Discipline: The Path to Spiritual Growth*, rev. ed. San Francisco: HarperSanFrancisco, 1988.

Friend, Howard E., Jr. *Recovering the Sacred Center: Church Renewal from the Inside Out*. Valley Forge, PA: Judson Press, 1998.

Green, Thomas H. *Weeds among the Wheat: Discernment: Where Prayer and Action Meet*. Notre Dame: Ave Maria Press, 1984.

Gula, Richard M. *Moral Discernment*. New York: Paulist Press, 1997.

Hahn, Celia Allison. *Uncovering Your Church's Hidden Spirit*. Bethesda, MD: Alban Institute, 2001.

Ignatius of Loyola, *The Spiritual Exercises of St. Ignatius*. Whitefish, MT: Kessinger Publishing, 2007.

Job, Rueben P., comp. *A Guide to Spiritual Discernment*. Nashville: Upper Room Books, 1996.

Jones, L. Gregory. *Embodying Forgiveness: A Theological Analysis*. Grand Rapids: William B. Eerdmans Publishing Company, 1995.

Keirsey, David, and Marilyn Bates. *Please Understand Me: Character and Temperament Types*. Del Mar, CA: Prometheus Nemesis Book Co., 1984.

McKinney, Mary Benet. *Sharing Wisdom: A Process for Group Decision Making*. Allen, TX: Thomas More, 1998.

Metz, Barbara, and John Burchill. *The Enneagram and Prayer: Discovering Our True Selves Before God*. Denville, NJ: Dimension Books, 1987.

Michael, Chester P., and Marie C. Norrisey. *Prayer and Temperament: Different Prayer Forms for Different Personality Types*. Charlottesville, VA: Open Door, 1984.

Morris, Danny E. *Yearning to Know God's Will: A Workbook for Discerning God's Guidance for Your Life*. Grand Rapids: Zondervan, 1991.

Morris, Danny E., and Charles M. Olsen. *Discerning God's Will Together: A Spiritual Practice for the Church*. Bethesda, MD: Alban Institute, 1997.

Morseth, Ellen. *Ritual & the Arts in Spiritual Discernment*. LaVergne, TN: Lightning Print, 1999.

Muller, Wayne. *Sabbath: Finding Rest, Renewal, and Delight in Our Busy Lives*. New York: Bantam Books, 2000.

Office of Theology and Worship Staff, *Book of Occasional Services: A Liturgical Resource Supplementing the Book of Common Worship*, 1993. Louisville: Geneva Press, 1999.

Olsen, Charles M. *Transforming Church Boards into Communities of Spiritual Leaders*. Bethesda, MD: Alban Institute, 1995.

Olsen, Charles M., and Ellen Morseth. *Selecting Church Leaders: A Practice in Spiritual Discernment*. Nashville: Upper Room, 2002.

Oswald, Roy M., and Robert E. Friedrich Jr. *Discerning Your Congregation's Future: A Strategic and Spiritual Approach*. Bethesda, MD: Alban Institute, 1996.

Presbyterian Church, Theology and Worship Ministry staff and the Cumberland Presbyterian Church staff. *Book of Common Worship, The*. Louisville, KY: Westminster John Knox Press, 1993.

Rendle, Gilbert R. *Behavioral Covenants in Congregations: A Handbook for Honoring Differences*. Bethesda, MD: Alban Institute, 1999.

Riso, Don Richard, and Russ Hudson. *The Wisdom of the Enneagram: The Complete Guide to Psychological and Spiritual Growth for the Nine Personality Types*. New York: Bantam Books, 1999.

Rogers, Frank, Jr. "Discernment," chapter 8 in *Practicing Our Faith: A Way of Life for a Searching People*, ed. Dorothy C. Bass. San Francisco: Jossey-Bass Publishers, 1997.

Simon, Sidney, Leland W. Howe, and Howard Kirschenbaum. *Values Clarification: A Practical, Action-Directed Workbook*, rev. ed. New York: Warner Books, 1995.

Standish, N. Graham. *Becoming a Blessed Church: Forming a Church of Spiritual Purpose, Presence, and Power*. Herndon, VA: Alban Institute, 2005.

Vennard, Jane E. *A Praying Congregation: The Art of Teaching Spiritual Practice*. Herndon, VA: Alban Institute, 2005.

Ware, Corinne. *Discover Your Spiritual Type: A Guide to Individual and Congregational Growth*. Bethesda, MD: Alban Institute, 1995.

Winner, Lauren F. *Mudhouse Sabbath: An Invitation to a Life of Spiritual Discipline*. Orleans, MA: Paraclete Press, 2007.

Winter, Miriam Therese. *WomanWisdom: A Feminist Lectionary and Psalter, Women of the Hebrew Scriptures: Part One*. New York: Crossroad Publishing Company, 1991.

Wolff, Pierre. *Discernment: The Art of Choosing Well*. rev ed. Liguori, MO: Liguori/Triumph Books, 2003.

Wright, Wendy M. "Passing Angels: The Arts of Spiritual Discernment," *Weavings: A Journal of the Christian Spiritual Life*, 10 no. 6 (Nov./Dec. 1995):6–15. Issue theme is "Discerning the Spirits."

Web sites:

Alban Institute: www.alban.org

Enneagram self test: www.enneagraminstitute.com

Lectionary: http://divinity.lib.vanderbilt.edu/lectionary

Music of Taizé: www.taize.fr/en

Myers-Briggs: www.personalitypathways.com/type_inventory.html

V. Isenhower Photography: www.visenhowerphotography.com

Water in the Desert Ministries

www.waterinthedesert.org